How Did Black History Month Begin?

Preserving The Legacy of African-American History

Michael A. Carson

Matthew A. Carson

Double Infinity Publishing
P. O. Box 55 Grayson, GA 30017

Printed in the United States of America

How Did Black History Month Begin?

Co-Author: Matthew A. Carson
Research Assistant: Matthew A. Carson
Content Editor: Shenika H. Carson
Cover Design: Double Infinity Publishing
Design Director: Shenika H. Carson

ISBN-979-8-9855087-0-3

Double Infinity Publishing books may be purchased in bulk at a special discount for sales promotion, corporate gifts, fund-raising or educational purposes. For details, contact the Special Sales Department, Double Infinity Publishing, P.O. Box 55 Grayson, GA. 30017 or by email: DoubleInfinityPublishing1@Gmail.com.

DEDICATION

As a Father and Son writing team, my co-author Matthew and I would like to dedicate this book to my beautiful wife Shenika, who continues to inspire us, thank you for all of your love and support.

To the next generation of African-American historians, writers and activists who continue to influence, inspire, and affect social change.

Other Publications By Author: Michael A. Carson

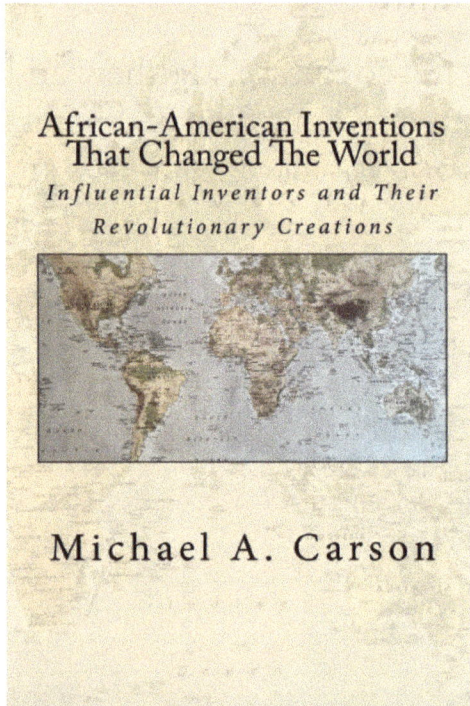

African-American Inventions That Changed The World

Influential Inventors and Their Revolutionary Creations

Michael A. Carson

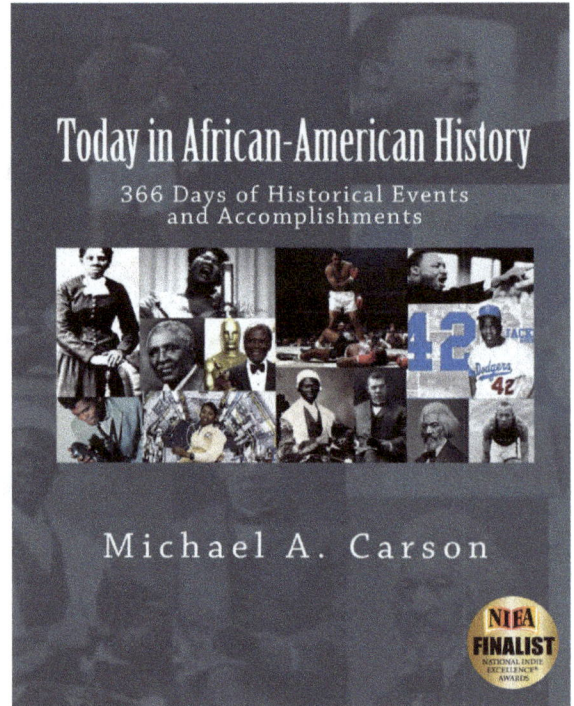

Today in African-American History

366 Days of Historical Events and Accomplishments

Michael A. Carson

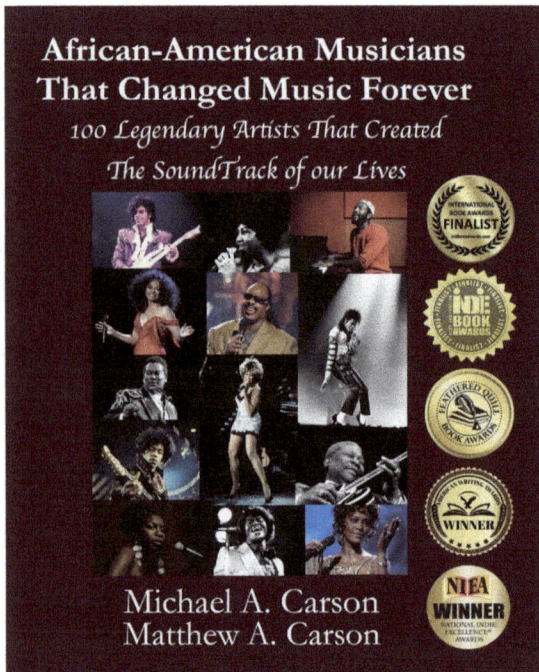

African-American Musicians That Changed Music Forever

100 Legendary Artists That Created The SoundTrack of our Lives

Michael A. Carson
Matthew A. Carson

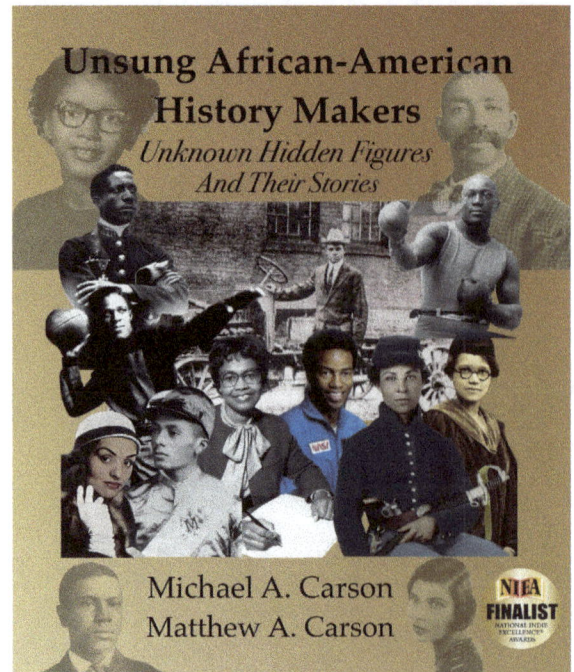

Unsung African-American History Makers

Unknown Hidden Figures And Their Stories

Michael A. Carson
Matthew A. Carson

Double Infinity Publishing

Contents

INTRODUCTION

The month of February has marked the celebration of Black History Month for more than half a century, an annual observance that recognizes and highlights the achievements and countless contributions of African-Americans. The yearly commemoration might not exist today if it were not for educator and historian, Dr. Carter G. Woodson, he devoted most of his life to shinning a light on the accomplishments of African-Americans throughout history.

Known as the Father of Black History, Woodson was motivated by contemporary historians who had tendencies to conceal historical contributions made by African-Americans from the history books. Throughout reconstruction until the early 20th century, many historians had a narrow scope in their historical narrative and their perspective was very limited on African-American contributions to society.

Woodson was fueled with a deep desire and determination to prove his predecessors wrong, he embarked on an educational journey to make the history of African-Americans both visible and appreciated. As a student of history, he was inspired by the stories he read over the years involving African-Americans who invented and accomplished things even while suffering extreme oppression. He published more than 20 books emphasizing the importance and power of the African-American story. Woodson was a true visionary, he did not let the obstacles and persecution he faced in his life stop him from becoming an esteemed groundbreaking writer and historian.

In 1926, he established an annual celebration known as Negro History Week, a commemoration during the second week of February to coincide with and pay homage to the birthdays of President Abraham Lincoln and Frederick Douglass, he credited the two with bringing an end to slavery in America. Negro History Week soon evolved into a monthly celebration in February known as Black History Month. The Federal Government officially recognized and began observing Black History Month in 1976 in conjunction with the Bicentennial Celebration.

"Real education means to inspire people to live more abundantly, to learn to begin with life as they find it and make it better."

*-- **Dr. Carter G. Woodson***

Chapter 1 - Dr. Carter G. Woodson

During the turn of the 20th Century, there were many obstacles for African-Americans living in America. The country overwhelmingly accepted and believed the notion that African-Americans did not contribute anything to society or world civilizations throughout history.

Those kind of distortions not only permeated the world of everyday Americans, but some deeply into the souls of African-Americans, if one was to believe these lies about their own people, how could they achieve the confidence to break the mold and have a different perspective of their history.

There were some who worked tirelessly to erase this false narrative and began to help people from all cultures to understand the true history of the African Diaspora experience in America and across the world.

The African-American community needed a rallying point to push their efforts and make people aware of all the many contributions that people of African descent made on the continent of Africa, The United States and across the globe.

Educator and historian, Dr. Carter G. Woodson dedicated his life to ensure all Americans heard a different side of the story, he strongly believed that hard facts through research and fair mindedness would bring balance to history, and all people throughout the world collectively made significant contributions to civilizations.

He realized once people on a mass scale understood this, there would be a greater respect for all ethnic backgrounds. Known today as the "Father of Black History," Woodson dedicated his career to the field of African-American history and lobbied extensively to establish a nationwide institution of learning.

"No man knows what he can do until he tries."

*-- **Dr. Carter G. Woodson***

Dr. Carter Godwin Woodson was born on December 19th 1875 in New Canton, Virginia, his story began in a similar fashion to the countless number of African-Americans who were coming of age during the difficult days of reconstruction. As the son of formerly enslaved Anne Eliza and James Henry Woodson, his parents were both illiterate and his father, who helped Union soldiers during the civil war, supported the family as a farmer.

While growing up on a farm, intensive field work often kept Woodson from attending primary school most days, he then sought to improve his standing with a relentless desire to learn, he devoted himself to the highest levels of education.

His family relocated to West Virginia when he was seventeen, he then began supporting himself by working in the coal mines, which left little or no time for pursuing an education.

A few years later, he saved enough money and enrolled himself into school at the age of twenty, he attended Frederick Douglass High School. Woodson was able to graduate within two years, he was later selected as the school's principal. Shortly after, he began working on his Bachelors Degree in Literature at Berea College in Kentucky, after graduation, he became a teacher and administrator there.

Woodson then traveled abroad, spending time teaching in the Philippines, while also visiting the Middle East and Europe, he later studied at Sorbonne University in Paris. When returning home to the U.S. he enrolled at the University of Chicago, receiving a second Bachelors Degree, then earning a Masters Degree in European History in 1908.

He then enrolled as a Doctoral student in History at Harvard University in Cambridge, Massachusetts. Woodson went on to graduate in 1912 earning his PhD in History, making him the second African-American (after W.E.B Du Bois) to earn a Doctorate Degree from Harvard.

In 1984, Dr. Carter G. Woodson was commemorated on the U.S. postage stamp. He is known as the "Father of Black History."

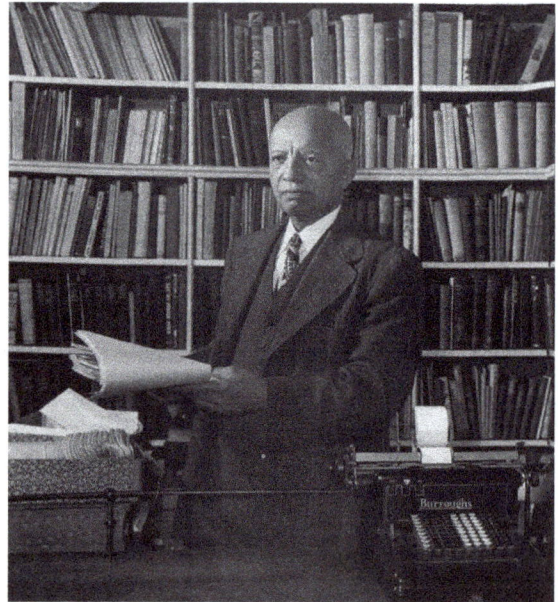

"Truth must be dug up from the past and presented to the circle of scholastics in scientific form and then through stories and dramatizations that will permeate our educational system."

-- Dr. Carter G. Woodson

Woodson later joined the faculty at Historically Black College and University (HBCU) Howard University in Washington D.C. where he served as a professor and Dean of the College of Arts and Sciences. Throughout his years traveling the world while being a student of history, he noticed many historians had a tendency to erase African-American stories and experiences from history books.

After graduating from a relatively progressive Harvard University, a motivated Woodson then embarked on an educational journey to make the history of African-Americans both visible and appreciated throughout the country. Contemporary historians during the time had a very narrow scope in their historical narratives, and their perspective on African-American history was very limited.

Woodson's determination to shine a light on his predecessor's stories solidified as he recalled many times when distinguished professors from his Harvard days informed students that African-Americans had no history in America and they did not contribute anything to society. Woodson was fueled with a deep seeded desire to prove them all wrong, as a scholar and student of history he knew of countless African-American men and women who contributed greatly to American history, particularly in the fields of education, science, technology, politics, law and medicine.

He knew what the impact and take away would be if students in school as well as everyday people began learning the stories of Phillis Wheatley's poems, Nat Turners revolt, Harriett Tubman's bravery, or how Frederick Douglass was one of the most influential men of the 19th century. He wanted African-Americans to began seeing how ordinary people could do extraordinary things, and how men and women just like them had the courage and determination to right a wrong and make it right.

In 1773, Phyllis Wheatley became the first African-American published author in the United States.

In 1831, Nat Turner lead the only effective slave rebellion in U.S. history.

Chapter 2 - Early Influencers

Woodson mentioned he was inspired by the stories he read over the years about the many unsung African-American figures who changed the course of history even while suffering extreme oppression. He included the story of Poet, Phillis Wheatley, who in 1773, became the first African-American published author in the United States, with her book "Poems on Various Subjects, Religious and Moral."

The publication brought her fame both in England and the American Colonies. Figures such as President George Washington praised her work, he personally told her that "the style and manner of your poetry exhibits a striking proof of your great poetical talents." Wheatley's poems also reflected pride in her African heritage, it was evident that her writing style embraced her African roots.

Woodson was also moved when he read the story about how Nat Turner lead the only effective slave rebellion in U.S. history in 1831. He learned that Turner inherited a passionate hatred of slavery from his African born mother, he saw himself as anointed by God to lead his people out of bondage. He took a solar eclipse as a sign that the time for revolution was near, and it began on August 21, 1831.

Turner and a small band of followers murdered his owners, the Travis family, then set off toward the town of Jerusalem, Virginia where they planned to capture an armory and gather more recruits. The rebels went from plantation to plantation, gathering horses and guns, freeing other slaves along the way as well recruiting others who wanted to join in what would later become one of the most effective revolts in U.S. history. As a scholar and historian, Woodson began an educational journey to pursue more information while also bringing awareness on these African-American figures who changed history.

In 1980, Inventor, Surveyor of Washington D.C. and creator the first clock ever built in the United States, Benjamin Banneker was commemorated on the U.S. postage stamp.

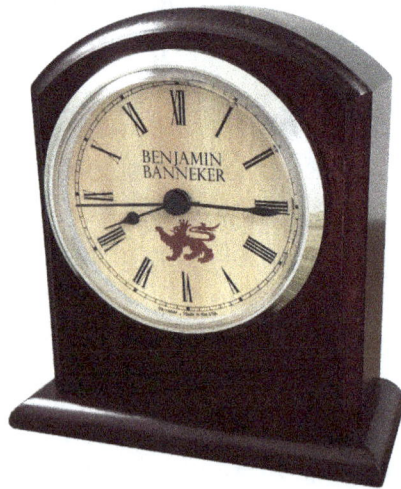

Woodson also had a great appreciation for African-American inventors. Although many from the early 1800's were born enslaved and not allowed to acquire a formal education, he realized these innovators made significant contributions to the world while faced with persecution and having to triumph over many adverse conditions.

Woodson learned about innovators such as Benjamin Banneker, who in 1753, invented the first clock in the United States at the age of twenty-one. At an early age, young Banneker was given a pocket watch as a gift, he was so fascinated by the object he repeatedly took the watch apart and then put it back together. He then read dozens of books on geometry and made plans to build a larger version of the watch.

After two years of designing and carving each piece by hand including the gears, Banneker successfully created the first clock ever built in the United States. The clock was amazingly precise and it kept perfect time for the next thirty years. He then later became a brilliant scientist and surveyor. In 1791, President George Washington made the decision to move the nation's capitol from Philadelphia to an area on the border of Maryland and Virginia.

He personally asked Banneker to assist with surveying and designing the territory, the plans and designs he drew up were the basis for the layout of Washington D.C. Many of the buildings and monuments he designed are still in existence today. Banneker's true acclaim also came from his almanacs, which he published for six consecutive years, between 1792 and 1797. After learning about Banneker and his contributions, Woodson was intrigued, he began researching more about the other incredible men and women inventors who changed and impacted our lives each day with their groundbreaking creations. He also learned that many African-American inventors were issued U.S. Patents for their creations and how their ingenuity changed the world.

In 1821, Thomas Jennings became the first African-American man to receive a U.S. patent for his invention of Dry Cleaning.

In 1887, Alexander Miles invented the modern day elevator. A new method of opening and closing elevator doors automatically.

During the 17th and 18th centuries, America was experiencing rapid economic growth. African-American inventors were major contributors during this era, even though most did not obtain any of the benefits associated with their inventions since they could not receive patent protection. In the early 1820's, U.S. patents were then issued to free African-Americans.

Patents were extremely important for the inventor, allowing them, if they wish, to earn money through sales or licensing of their product. Since then, African-American inventors have made major significant contributions to the world with their creativity and innovation.

Thomas Jennings became the first African-American man in the country to receive a U.S. patent, in 1821, he invented Dry Cleaning. His invention began as he experimented with different cleaning agents and solutions, he tested them on various fabrics until he found the right combination to effectively clean them.

His method of cleaning garments with an organic solvent that doesn't include water has stood the test of time for the past two centuries. The dry-cleaning business continues to be the cornerstone of all neighborhoods in every major city worldwide.

Alexander Miles was another prolific inventor that Woodson admired, in 1887, he invented the modern day elevator. Earlier elevator models were not designed for passenger safety, if someone failed to close the door leading to the shaft when exiting, another passenger could possibly fall down the shaft while attempting to step into the elevator.

Miles realized the daily imminent danger his children and others faced associated with an elevator shaft door being carelessly left open, this event inspired him to draft a design for automated elevator doors. He invented and patented an automated mechanism that allowed shaft doors along with the elevator doors to open and close automatically on each floor. This new method and design would forever revolutionize how elevators would be used for generations to come and greatly increase passenger safety.

"If women want any rights more than they got, why don't they just take them, and not be talking about it."

-- Sojourner Truth

In 1986, Abolitionist and Women's Rights Activist Sojourner Truth was commemorated on the U.S. postage stamp.

Sojourner Truth
22

Black Heritage USA

Unlike many other historians of the time, Woodson firmly believed African-American women played a major role in shaping American history, he was fascinated by the story of Sojourner Truth. As an abolitionist and woman's rights activist, Truth addressed the first Black Women's Rights Convention in Akron, Ohio in 1851. Her famous speech titled "Ain't I a Woman?" was a landmark moment in feminist and abolitionist history.

Originally bearing the name Isabella Baumfree, in 1793, Truth was born as an enslaved person before escaping with her infant daughter to freedom in 1826. Moving to New York City in 1828, she joined a local church, she then participated in the religious revivals throughout the state and became a charismatic speaker. She was convinced the Lord gave her the name Sojourner Truth, as he called upon her to "travel up and down the land declaring the truth to people."

Truth was the guest of President Lincoln at the White House on several occasions and was one of the voices that influenced Lincoln to recruit African-American soldiers for the Union Army during the civil war. She was a powerful and impassioned speaker whose legacy of feminism and racial equality still resonates today.

As one of the world's best-known human rights crusaders, Truth dedicated her life to fighting for a more equal society for African-Americans and for women. Her passions including abolition, voting rights, and property rights. In 1844, Truth joined the Northampton Association of Education and Industry in Northampton, MA. The organization supported a broad reform agenda including women's rights and pacifism.

Along with Frederick Douglass and Harriett Tubman, Truth was one of several escaped enslaved people to rise to prominence as an abolitionist leader, and a testament to the humanity of enslaved people. In 2009, she became the first African-American woman to have a bronze sculpture in her honor on display inside the U.S. Capitol, the over-life-size bust displays Truth in her cap and shawl.

Frederick Douglass

In 1995, Abolitionist, Author, Orator and perhaps the most influential man of the 19th century, Frederick Douglass was commemorated on the U.S. postage stamp.

In 1995, Abolitionist and famous Conductor of the Underground Railroad, Harriet Tubman was also commemorated on the U.S. postage stamp.

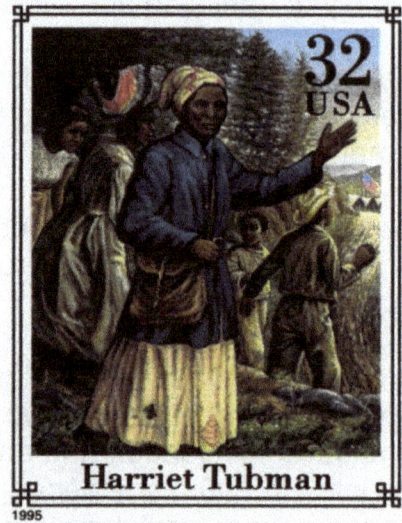

Harriet Tubman

As one of the most influential figures of the 19th century, Frederick Douglass was someone that Woodson really admired. As the Civil War developed, Douglass convinced President Abraham Lincoln to free all enslaved people so they may enlist in Union Forces, the Emancipation Proclamation was issued and Douglass became one of the main recruiters of free African-American soldiers in the Northern territories.

Born into slavery, Douglass escaped at the age of twenty and went on to become a world renowned anti-slavery activist. After his escape from Maryland, he became a national leader of the abolitionist movement and began gaining notoriety for public speaking. As an abolitionist, author and orator, Douglass then became the first African-American to be nominated as a U.S. Presidential Candidate in 1888.

He also became the first African-American federal U.S. Marshal, his jurisdiction was the District of Columbia. While occupying this position, Douglass continued to strengthen the hold of African-American civil servants in governmental positions in the Nation's Capital, he often worked closely with fellow abolitionist Harriett Tubman.

As the most famous conductor of the underground railroad, Tubman travelled nearly 90 miles on her journey for freedom from Maryland to Philadelphia, she bravely returned back later to Maryland in order to rescue members of her family. She made more than a dozen trips back to Maryland over an eleven year period, she successfully led more than 300 people out of bondage to their freedom heading North.

Tubman was someone Woodson had a great admiration for due to her bravery. He learned she was a spy, nurse, and scout for the United States Army during the American Civil War. She also became the only woman during the war to carry out an armed expedition and raid enemy forces along the Combahee River in South Carolina. Due to the raid, she helped to free more than 750 enslaved people. In 2016, the U.S. Department of Treasury announced that Tubman will be the first African-American person to appear on a U.S. currency note, her photo will be displayed on the twenty dollar bill.

The First Black Members of the U.S. Congress

During the early 1870's (5 years before he was born) Woodson also learned that more than a dozen African-American men, many of whom had been born into slavery, were elected to the U.S. Congress. During the reconstruction era, the first African-Americans to serve in the Congress were elected after the 13th and 14th Amendments to the Constitution granted freedom and citizenship to enslaved people.

In 1870, Hiram Revels became the first African-American elected to serve in the United States Senate, he represented the State of Mississippi. He became an outspoken opponent to racial segregation and he broke new ground for African-Americans in politics. Newly free men gained political representation in the Southern States for the first time. The 15th Amendment guaranteed citizens the right to vote, in response there were a growing number of African-American politicians.

Woodson estimated about two thousand African-Americans held some kind of public office during Reconstruction, these pioneering representatives symbolized a new democratic order in the United States. While demonstrating both courage and determination, they often braved elections marred by violence and fraud, nevertheless in the House they argued passionately for civil rights and equality.

In 1874, the U.S. Congress debated a new civil rights law that would outlaw discrimination based on race in hotels, theaters, and railway cars. Along with the votes of the newly elected African-American Congressmen, the civil rights law passed, President Ulysses S. Grant signed it into law and it was enacted on March 1, 1875.

The new civil rights act affirmed the "equality of all men before the law" and prohibited racial discrimination in public places and facilities such as restaurants and public transportation. All lawsuits arising under the new law were to be tried in federal courts, rather than at the state level.

In 1879, Mary Eliza Mahoney graduated from the Nursing program at the New England Hospital for Women and Children, she became the first African-American registered nurse in the United States.

As more civil rights laws were being passed by Congress during the mid-1870's granting equality to African-Americans, there were a number of African-American women who were also fighting for their social and civil rights as well. The New England Hospital for Women and Children operated one of the first nursing schools in the United States.

In 1878, a thirty-three year old nursing student named Mary Eliza Mahoney was admitted to the hospital's professional graduate school for nursing. The program, which ran for 16 months, was intensive. Each student attended lectures and gained first-hand experience in the hospital, of the 42 students that entered the program in 1878, only 4 completed it in 1879. Mahoney was one of the women who completed the program, making her the first African-American registered nurse in the United States.

After earning her professional nursing license, Mahoney was an active participant in the nursing profession, she worked for many years as a private care nurse, earning a distinguished reputation. Her professionalism helped raise the status and standards of all nurses, especially minorities, she received private-duty nursing requests from patients in states in the North, South and East coast.

In 1896, Mahoney became an original founding member of the predominantly Caucasian "Nurses Associated Alumnae of the United States and Canada" (NAAUSC). In the early 1900's, the NAAUSC did not welcome African-American nurses, while Mahoney began to encounter overwhelming discrimination from other nurses.

In response, she founded a new, more welcoming nursing association. In 1908, Mahoney founded the National Association of Colored Graduate Nurses (NACGN). The NACGN had a significant influence on eliminating racial discrimination in the registered nursing profession.

In 1951, the NACGN merged with the American Nurses Association (ANA). As a pioneer in nursing, Mahoney was inducted into the American Nurses Association Hall of Fame in 1976, and to the National Women's Hall of Fame in 1993.

As the founder of Tuskegee Institute, *Booker T. Washington was one of the most influential African-American intellectuals of the late 19th Century.*

In 1940, he became the first African-American commemorated on a U.S. Postal Stamp.

In 1946, he also became the first African-American featured on a U.S. Coin, the half-dollar, featured the bust of Washington.

In 1948, Inventor and Botanist, George Washington Carver was commemorated on the U.S. postage stamp. Known as the "Plant Doctor," he famously developed more than 500 uses from peanuts, soybeans and sweet potatoes.

Chapter 3 - Coming of Age

During the early 1900's, segregation took an even stronger hold in the South, many African-Americans including Woodson saw self-improvement, especially through education, as the single greatest opportunity to escape the indignities they suffered. Many looked to prominent educator, Booker T. Washington, a formally enslaved author of the bestselling book "Up From Slavery" (1900), as an inspiration.

Washington rose to become one of the most influential African-American intellectuals of the late 19th Century. In 1881, he founded Tuskegee Institute, a Historically Black College and University (HBCU) in Alabama that was devoted to training teachers. Washington was also behind the formation of the National Negro Business League. He later served as an adviser to Presidents Theodore Roosevelt and William Howard Taft.

Washington urged African-Americans to acquire the kind of industrial or vocational training (such as farming and mechanics) that would give them the necessary skills to carve out a niche for themselves in the U.S. economy. Washington also recruited George Washington Carver, another formerly enslaved man to head Tuskegee's agriculture department, Carver single handedly liberated the South from its reliance of cotton by convincing farmers to plant peanuts and soybeans each year in order to rejuvenate the exhausted soil each season.

Carver revolutionized agriculture in the Southern region of the United States, transforming its economy. As a world renown inventor, he also developed hundreds of uses from peanut oil, including soap, medicines, insecticides and plastic to name a few. He also taught automotive pioneer Henry Ford how to construct automobile parts using plastic that was produced from soybeans. Known as the "Plant Doctor," Carver also taught Ford and his engineers how to mass produce more than one automobile at a time on an assembly line. Due to his teachings, mass production facilities all over the world then became known as the "Plant."

W.E.B. Du Bois was commemorated on the U.S. postage stamp in 1992, he is known for being one of the founders of the National Association for the Advancement of Colored People (NAACP) in 1909.

Journalist, Educator and an early leader in the Civil Rights Movement, Ida B. Wells was commemorated on the U.S. postage stamp in 1990. Wells was also one of the founders of the NAACP in 1909.

During the early 20th century, Woodson also greatly admired the civil rights activists who tirelessly fought for equal rights for African-Americans, including historian W.E.B. Du Bois (William Edward Burghardt) and women's rights activist, Ida B. Wells.

In 1895, Du Bois became the first African-American to earn a Ph.D. from Harvard University, he then rose to national prominence as a leader of the Niagara Movement, a civil rights organization founded in 1905. Wells owned a newspaper called "Memphis Free Speech and Headlight," she was active in the women's rights and women's suffrage movements, establishing several notable women's organizations.

Together Du Bois and Wells were perhaps best known for their work in becoming the founders of The "National Association for the Advancement of Colored People" (NAACP), the organization was founded on the 100th anniversary of President Abraham Lincoln's birthday, February 12, 1909. The mission of the NAACP is to ensure the political, educational, social, and economic equality of rights of all people and to eliminate discrimination. The NAACP has become the oldest and largest grassroots civil rights organization in U.S. history.

In 1917, Du Bois, Wells and James Weldon Johnson (writer of the lyrics for the song, "Lift Every Voice and Sing" which became known as the "Black National Anthem") led ten thousand African-Americans to march down New York City's 5th Avenue in an NAACP organized protest against lynchings, discrimination and the denial of civil rights.

This was the first major civil rights demonstration of the 20th Century. The march was a major turning point, Wells became one of the most famous African-American women in the United States during the era, she dedicated her life to combating racial injustice and violence against African-Americans, she also fought for the equality of all women.

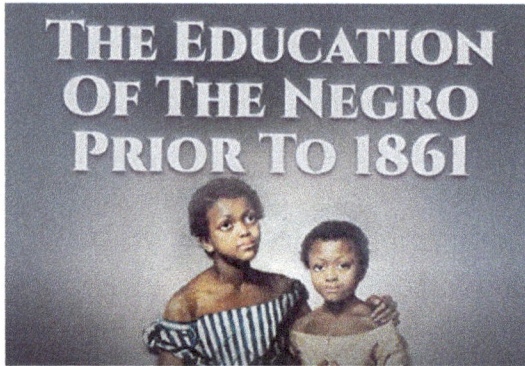

In 1915, Dr. Carter G. Woodson wrote and published his first book, "The Education of the Negro Prior to 1861."

In 1915, he also founded the Association for the Study of Negro Life and History, now called the Association for the Study of African-American Life and History (ASALH).

Chapter 4 - The Education of the Negro Prior to 1861

After learning about the countless contributions that African-Americans made in our society and the world, in 1915, while serving as a professor and Dean of the College of Arts and Sciences at Howard University, Woodson wrote and published his first book, "The Education of the Negro Prior to 1861." This book served as a pivotal publication that addressed African-American history, a subject he felt was badly neglected and crudely misrepresented by other educators.

The book emphasized the importance and power of the African-American story in America and abroad. Woodson detailed why African-American history was not being taught during the time, he also explained how historically enslavers were responsible for preventing enslaved people from receiving proper education in order to easily force them into subordination. He further argued the perpetuation of this practice to erase African-American history has benefited oppressors for centuries.

Woodson felt the only way to effectively fight racism is to educate the African-American community about their heritage, and teach them about the many contributions African-Americans have made in American and world societies, this would break the stigma of their race being regarded as inferior.

While researching the topics for this book, Woodson mentioned in the preface that he was particularly inspired by the stories he read and heard over the years about the many heroic African-Americans who overcame extreme oppression, and later became world renown figures.

In 1915, Woodson also founded the "Association for the Study of Negro Life and History." This organization created research and publication outlets for African-American scholars, the organization later established of "The Journal of Negro History" (1916) and "The Negro History Bulletin" (1937), which both garnered a popular public appeal.

In 2002, Langston Hughes was commemorated on the U.S. postage stamp. He was one of the earliest innovators of the literary art form called Jazz poetry, and best known as a leader of the Harlem Renaissance. Hughes published more than 35 books, and his influence is seen in the writings of authors from his generation to the present.

In 2020, Philosopher, writer, and educator, Alain Locke was commemorated on the U.S. Postage stamp. He is the first African-American Rhodes Scholar, and is heralded as the "Father of the Harlem Renaissance."

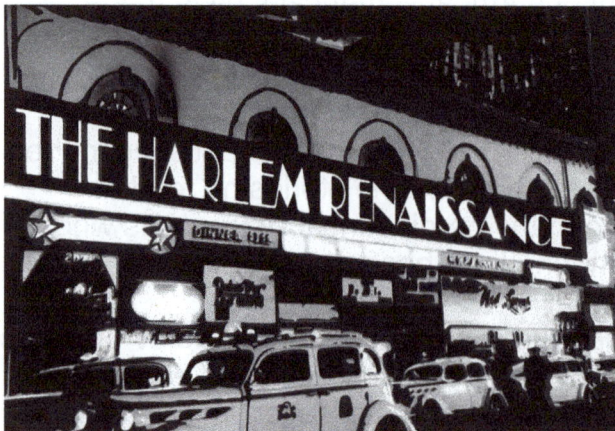

Chapter 5 - Raising Awareness

Woodson's ongoing quest of raising awareness and making it accessible to others continued during the early 1920's, he noticed a great migration of African-Americans from the rural South to the urban North sparked a cultural renaissance that took place in the New York City neighborhood of Harlem and became a widespread movement throughout the country.

Known originally as "The New Negro Movement," "The Harlem Renaissance" marked the first time mainstream publishers turned their attention seriously to African-American literature, music, art and politics.

This cultural movement was greatly stimulated by the weekly journals Woodson published which detailed African-American history. The NAACP and the National Urban League also published short pieces by promising writers during the time.

This movement gave great exposure to Woodson and also popularized other emerging African-American writers at the time such as Alain Locke, a Howard University Chair and the first African-American Rhodes Scholar who was heralded as the "Father of the Harlem Renaissance" for his 1925 publication of "The New Negro."

Poet, Langston Hughes also had one of the leading voices in the Harlem Renaissance, his poems embraced radical politics, poverty, prejudice, violence, and a host of other socio-economic issues that chronicle the African-American experience during the time.

The influence of the movement stretched around the world, opening the doors of mainstream culture to African-American artists and writers. Bandleader Louis Armstrong, Blues singer Bessie Smith, composer Duke Ellington, and actress Josephine Baker were among the leading entertainment talents during the Harlem Renaissance.

BLACK HERITAGE

USA 32

BESSIE COLEMAN

In 1995, Bessie Coleman was commemorated on the U.S. postage stamp. She was the first African-American woman to earn a pilot license.

"I refused to take no for an answer."

-- *Bessie Coleman*

While Woodson was continuing his quest to bring awareness during this new cultural movement of the 1920's, there were a number of trailblazing African-American pioneers who were making their own history during the time. Bessie Coleman began her journey as a young woman growing up in Atlanta, Texas.

At the age of twenty-three, she became intrigued by the stories she heard from pilots who returned home from their tour of duty in World War I, who detailed their experiences flying planes on missions during the war.

Coleman later relocated to Chicago where she became interested in enrolling in an aviation school in order to earn her pilots license. Due to racial and gender discrimination during the time, all aviation schools in the United States denied her entry.

Founder and publisher of the Chicago Defender, Robert S. Abbott, encouraged her to study abroad. He publicized Coleman's quest in his newspaper and she received financial sponsorship from banker, Jesse Binga (A prominent businessman who founded the first privately owned African-American bank in Chicago).

Coleman took a French language class in Chicago before traveling to Paris, France to attend "The Caudron Brother's School of Aviation" where she was taught how to fly and maneuver planes by french pilots. In 1921, she became the first African-American woman to earn a pilot license, a personal goal she accomplished in only seven months.

Popularly known as "Queen Bess" she returned to the United States as a licensed pilot. As the age of commercial flying being a decade in the future, Coleman earned a living as a civilian aviator known as a "barnstorming" flier (A pilot who performs aerial tricks for thousands of spectators). She often performed heart thrilling stunts for as many as 3,000 people, including local dignitaries who attended the event. Coleman often used her position of prominence to encourage others to fly. She remains a pioneer in the field of Aviation, serving as an inspiration for several generations of African-American aspiring pilots.

As one of the most influential inventors of the 1920's, Garrett Morgan invented the Traffic Signal and Gas Mask. His safety inventions have improved and saved countless lives worldwide, including firefighters, miners, soldiers and vehicle operators.

"If you want to do something, then be the best."

*-- **Garrett Morgan***

Garrett Morgan was another trailblazing pioneer who Woodson highlighted in his weekly journal during the time, as he emerged as one of the most influential inventors of the early 20th century. Growing up in Paris, Kentucky, Morgan changed the course of history with his revolutionary creations.

In 1914, he invented a breathing device called the "Safety Hood," which provided a safer breathing experience in the presence of smoke, gases and other pollutants. He was inspired to create and patent this device after witnessing a devastating fire that engulfed a factory building. He noticed firefighters struggling to protect themselves against the suffocating smoke while trying to contain the fire.

Morgan's breathing device became a prototype and the precursor for the gas masks used during World War I, protecting soldiers from toxic gas used during warfare. His invention was famously put to use during a tragic event in Cleveland, Ohio.

In 1916, a tunnel that was being drilled under Lake Erie suddenly collapsed, trapping 32 workers. Smoke and toxic fumes prevented firefighters from safely rescuing the workers. Morgan along with his brother used his safety hood to successfully reach the trapped men and safely rescue several survivors.

In 1923, Morgan also invented the modern day Traffic Signal, he was inspired to do so after he witnessed a traffic collision between an automobile and a horse and carriage. His new traffic signal was the first to feature three commands instead of two, which controlled traffic more effectively. In 1923, he sold the patent rights to General Electric for $40,000.00. His inventions improved and saved countless lives worldwide, including firefighters, soldiers and vehicle operators.

Morgan also supported the African-American community throughout his lifetime, he was an active member of the NAACP and donated money to Historically Black Colleges and Universities (HBCU's). In 1920, he also launched an African-American newspaper, named after his hometown "The Cleveland Call."

In the early 1920's, the Greenwood District of Tulsa, Oklahoma became one of the most prominent concentrations of African-American businesses in the United States, local residents collectively funneled their cash into their own local economy. By 1921, the city was home to more than 10,000 African-American residents.

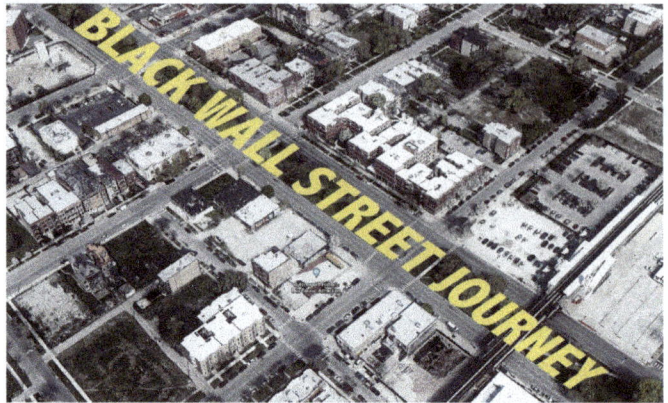

Woodson also highlighted in his weekly journal the number of communities in the country that was thriving with African-American entrepreneurial businesses. The prosperous town of Tulsa, Oklahoma, which was founded by many descendants of enslaved people, earned a reputation of what educator, Booker T. Washington called the "Black Wall Street of America."

In the early 1920's, the Greenwood District of Tulsa became one of the most prominent concentrations of African-American businesses in the United States, local residents collectively funneled their cash into their own local businesses.

Greenwood became a robust and self-sustaining community, which prominently featured over 600 businesses including, 21 churches 2 movie theaters, 30 grocery stores, 21 restaurants, 6 private planes, hospitals, banks, schools, libraries, post office, and bus system. All of these businesses were exclusively owned and operated by African-Americans.

On Black Wall Street, there were attorneys, entrepreneurs, doctors, real estate agents, and barbers who offered their services in the neighborhood, which soon became one of the most commercially successful and affluent majority African-American communities in the country during the time.

Greenwood also appealed to African-American southerners who migrated to the North and West in hopes of escaping the economic and political repression which they experienced in the South. Many of them relocated to Tulsa and soon created an even more prosperous community in Greenwood. By 1921, the city was home to more than 10,000 African-American residents.

Greenwood residents selected their own leaders and raised capital to support economic growth. There was also three African-American millionaires living in Greenwood during the time, in the surrounding area of northeastern Oklahoma, they enjoyed relative prosperity and participated in the oil boom.

In 1995, Madam C.J. Walker was commemorated on the U.S. postage stamp. She was the first woman in the United States to become a self-made millionaire.

"If I have accomplished anything in life, it is because I have been willing to work hard. Don't sit down and wait for the opportunities to come. Get up and make them."

-- Madam C.J. Walker

As Woodson's weekly journal gained popularity throughout many parts of the country, he often published stories about entrepreneur and businesswoman Madam C.J. Walker. Walker became one of the most successful and powerful influencers of the early 20th century, building an empire and creating a line of extremely popular hair care and beauty products for African-Americans.

Born in Delta, Louisiana as Sarah Breedlove, Walker did not have a formal education growing up, she mostly worked as a laborer until her early twenties, often earning as little as $1.50 per day. In the 1890's, she began to notice places on her scalp where she was losing her hair, which was not rare among women during that time.

Walker began experimenting with homemade treatments by mixing items from her local drugstore, she eventually created a scalp conditioning and healing formula that worked for her. She named her new formula, "Madame C.J. Walker's Wonderful Hair Grower."

Walker then enrolled at Poro College (A school which focused on helping African-American women learn about hair and skin care to create their own beauty care businesses).

In 1906, she changed her name to Madam C.J. Walker and marketed herself as an independent hairdresser and retailer of cosmetic creams. She adopted the name "Madam" from women pioneers of the French Beauty Industry.

Walker built a business empire, traveling around the country promoting her products door-to-door along with hair care tips to African-American women. She also employed hundreds of "beauty culturalists" to hand-sell her products. Her savvy talent for self-promotion made her one of the most famous African-Americans of her time and a very successful businesswoman.

She was also the first woman in the United States to become a self-made millionaire. She used her fortune to fund scholarships for women at the Tuskegee Institute and donated large parts of her wealth to the NAACP, the YMCA and other charities.

After years of conducting research on African-American historical figures along with their accomplishments, Dr. Carter G. Woodson and his organization, the Association for the Study of African-American Life and History (ASALH) decided it was time to share what they learned with others. In 1926, he established an annual celebration known as "Negro History Week," a commemoration during the second week of February to coincide with and pay homage to the birthdays of President Abraham Lincoln and Frederick Douglass, he credited the two with bringing an end to slavery in America. Negro History Week soon evolved into a monthly celebration in February known as Black History Month. The Federal Government officially recognized and began observing Black History Month in 1976 in conjunction with the Bicentennial Celebration.

Chapter 6 - Negro History Week

In 1923, Woodson began drafting and circulating a pamphlet promoting Negro History Week. He urged Historically Black Colleges and Universities (HBCU's) and their students to began exploring ways to celebrate their heritage by researching African-American historical figures along with their accomplishments. His fraternity brothers from Omega Psi Phi responded with the creation of Negro History and Literature Week in 1924.

Woodson soon took the idea to the next level in 1926 when he pioneered the celebration of Negro History Week. He dedicated the second week in February to coincide with and pay homage to the birthdays of President Abraham Lincoln and Frederick Douglass, he credited the two with bringing an end to slavery in America.

He would herald the celebration in his Negro History Week pamphlets causing a stir in the direction of active participation as he mailed them to several Historically Black Colleges and Universities, radio stations, civic organizations, and literary societies.

Woodson would began offering promotional materials to those who agreed to take up the celebration as well as guidance on how to shape such festivities. He was soon overwhelmed by the response to his call, teachers from all across the country endorsed his efforts and began asking for more materials to instruct their pupils.

Negro History Week gained popularity with help from teachers and church leaders. Early Negro History Week celebrations included banquets, speeches, parades and lectures, many of which were free for the public to attend. Several African-American owned newspapers also hopped onboard as they printed articles about the annual observance. The "Chicago Defenders," "The Cleveland Call," "Philadelphia Tribune" and "Tampa Bulletin" were amongst the largest and early supporters of the movement.

"Those who have no record of what their forebears have accomplished, lose the inspiration which comes from the teaching of biography and history."

-- Dr. Carter G. Woodson

While still serving as the dean of the School of Liberal Arts at Howard University, Woodson realized that his organization, the Association for the Study of Negro Life and History, now called the Association for the Study of African-American Life and History (ASALH) needed his undivided attention. In 1935, he decided to retire from the university, although he never officially retired from educating the masses.

Negro History Week became a main stay in areas with major African-American populations such as New York City, Detroit, Chicago, and Washington D.C. as well as smaller communities in the South. As more teachers endorsed his efforts across the country, Woodson and the ASALH scrambled to meet the demand. Along with a steady flow of knowledge, high schools in progressive communities began to form Negro History Clubs.

The ASALH formed branches that stretched from coast to coast. In 1937, at the urging of his friend and fellow educator, Mary McLeod Bethune, Woodson established the Negro History Bulletin, in order to focus on the annual theme of Negro History Week.

The publication proved more accessible to the working class which had a wider and more relatable reach than his scholarly journal. As African-American populations grew in more cities, many mayors began to issue Negro History Week proclamations.

Woodson was not satisfied with the celebration being limited to seven days out of the year. He hoped that Negro History Week would spark the development of a massive curriculum on African-American studies amongst schools around the country. He believed that education along with increasing social and professional contexts among African-American and Caucasian people could significantly reduce racism and prejudices.

Negro History Week proved to be a dynamic force during the 1940's, the movement became an intellectual insurgency that was part of a larger effort to transform race relations in America. Efforts slowly began to expand African-American history to schools nationwide.

"Those who endeavor to understand their own history are paving a path towards a brighter future."

-- Dr. Carter G. Woodson

"We have a powerful potential in our youth, and we must have the courage to change old ideas and practices so that we may direct their power toward good ends."

-- Dr. Mary McLeod Bethune

Woodson devoted much of his life to historical research and work to preserve the history of African-Americans as he accumulated a collection of thousands of publications and artifacts. Along his journey, fellow educator, Dr. Mary McLeod Bethune was instrumental in helping him establish Negro History Week.

While both living in Washington, D.C. Bethune and Woodson shared a friendship as they had much in common. As educators, they had a shared passion for shaping the minds of their many young African-Americans students.

Similar to Woodson, Bethune believed traditional historians had little or no interest in African-American history, as their contributions were overlooked, ignored, and even suppressed by the writers of history textbooks and the teachers who use them.

Bethune became the first female president of the Association for the Study of African-American Life and History (ASALH), and with the help of Woodson, the pair created "The Negro Bulletin."

While his other publication "The Journal of Negro History" was already popular, both educators wanted something that would be easily accessible for everyday people, especially teachers and young students.

The organization not only produced scholarly monographs, but also collected and published primary research materials that other scholars could use. Woodson realized that he had a major responsibility to preserve historical as well as contemporary documentation on the African-American experience for future generations.

He was determined to change and correct the racist biases that plagued historical work about the African-American experience and their role in American history. One of his highest priorities was breaking with the misconception that African-American people did not contribute anything to society, but instead shining a light on their more important and active roles in American history.

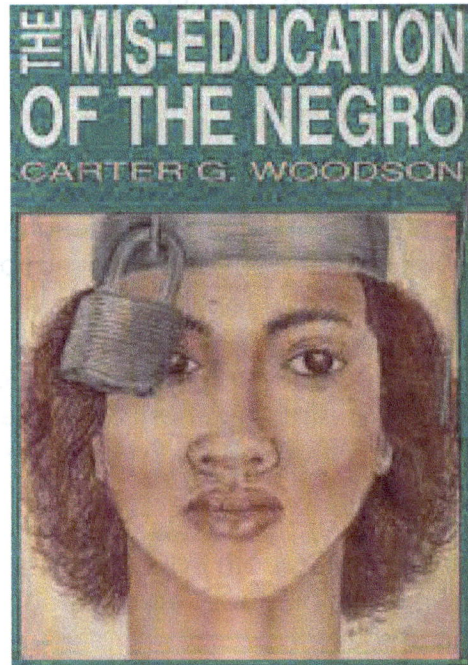

"When you control a man's thinking, you do not have to worry about his actions. You do not have to tell him not to stand here or go yonder. He will find his 'proper place' and will stay in it. You do not need to send him to the back door. He will go without being told. In fact, if there is no back door, he will protest until one is made for his use. His education makes it necessary."

-- Dr. Carter G. Woodson

Chapter 7 - The Mis-Education of The Negro

In 1933, Woodson published his next book "The Mis-Education of The Negro," which was a historical and extremely important critique of the American education system. The thesis of this book was that African-American students of his day were being culturally indoctrinated rather than taught in American schools.

He felt this conditioning caused African-American people to become dependent, and they would seek out inferior positions in the greater American society. The most crucial element in his concept which he highlighted in the book hinged on the education system failure to present authentic African-American history in school curriculum.

Woodson found his voice with this sophisticated critique of a post civil war education system that was more focused on training African-American students to work instead of educating or empowering them to excel. He highlighted America's neglect and intentional way of teaching, and the many historians who were not genuine in providing an accurate account of America's history, that did not include the significant contributions from the African-American community but also not acknowledging the pains, struggles and history of slavery.

His constructive critique gave a lesson on how improving the lives of the poor has to be accomplished by change being radical and practical, he also stated in his most famous quote, "When you control a man's thinking, you do not have to worry about his actions." This book would go on to change the scope of the United States educational system for decades to come, and would later become a required reading for many colleges and universities across the country. The Mis-Education of the Negro is one of the most important and best-selling books ever written on the subject of education. Woodson challenged his readers to become "self-taught" and to "do for themselves," regardless of what they were taught by others.

Mary McLeod Bethune

Black Heritage USA 22

In 1985, Dr. Mary McLeod Bethune was commemorated on the U.S. postage stamp. As an educator and activist, she served as President of the Association for the Study of African-American Life and History, the National Association of Colored Women, and founder of the National Council of Negro Women. She started a private school for African-American students in Daytona Beach, Florida, which later developed as Bethune-Cookman University. Bethune was also an Adviser to President Franklin D. Roosevelt.

Dr. Mary McLeod Bethune
1875-1935

MM00000

South Carolina

She was also the first African-American woman commemorated on a license plate issued by the state of South Carolina, where her photo is proudly displayed.

MARY McLEOD BETHUNE

Chapter 8 - Breaking Through Barriers

While assisting with a successful launch of Negro History Week, Dr. Mary McLeod Bethune also emerged as one of the most influential educators and civil rights figures of the early 20th century. While living in Washington D.C., she got married and later relocated to Florida, as she often dreamt of opening her own school for African-American girls.

Along with her faith in God, she enlisted the help of her local church, and her community in order to opened the Daytona Literary and Industrial Training School for Negro Girls with only $1.50 and five little girls. In 1923, her school merged with Cookman Institute of Jacksonville and became co-ed, the name then officially changed to Bethune-Cookman University, as Bethune became the first president.

She used the university as a base to become involved with women's rights, politics, and civil rights. During World War II, Bethune became close personal friends of President Franklin D. Roosevelt and his wife Eleanor, she was invited to the White House to join his cabinet as an adviser. She also became the first African-American woman to head a federal office, serving as Director of the Division of Minority Affairs, an advisory board to the Roosevelt administration on issues facing African-Americans in America.

In 1935, Bethune founded the National Council of Negro Women (NCNW), which spearheaded strategies and developed programs that advanced the interests of African-American women. She also co-founded the United Negro College Fund (UNCF), a philanthropic organization that funds scholarships for African-American students. In 1974, a monument honoring the life and contribution of Bethune was built in Washington, D.C., this was the first statue of an African-American erected on public land in the Nation's Capital. Her homes in Washington D.C. and Daytona Beach, FL., also became historic landmarks.

In 2010, Baseball Player, Andrew "Rube" Foster was commemorated on the U.S. postage stamp. Known as the "Father of the Negro Leagues, he organized the first successful African-American Professional Baseball League in 1920.

Since the inception of Woodson's annual observance of Negro History Week in 1926, each year began a new chapter of African-American figures that were becoming more mainstream across the country. Known as a "national pastime," professional baseball became the dominant sport during the early 20th century, and several professional leagues were being formed across the country. Major League Baseball barred African-Americans players from participation on teams along with Caucasian players due to their race and the rise of segregation.

Although many great African-American players did play on small regional teams, a major turning point came in 1920, when Andrew "Rube" Foster founded a new league for African-American players called the Negro National League.

The league was launched with eight teams, Chicago American Giants, Chicago Giants, Cuban Stars, Dayton Marcos, Detroit Stars, Kansas City Monarchs, Indianapolis ABC's and the St. Louis Giants.

The league discovered financial success coming out of the gate, all teams combined drew a crowd of nearly 200,000 spectators during its inaugural 1920 season. The Negro National League created a forum where many star players could make a bigger name for themselves, especially to Caucasian audiences.

Future Hall of Famers, Cool Papa Bell, Judy Johnson, and Satchel Paige all flourished in the Negro National League, along with many others. As the "Father of the Negro Leagues," Foster was inducted to the Baseball Hall of Fame in 1981.

The National Negro league would continue a full-time and robust operation until one of its own, a Kansas City Monarchs player named Jackie Robinson broke Major League Baseball's color barrier in 1947. In 2020, Major League Baseball announced that it was classifying all Negro League players as Major Leagues players, recognizing all statistics from the approximately 3,400 players who played during the era from 1920 until 1948.

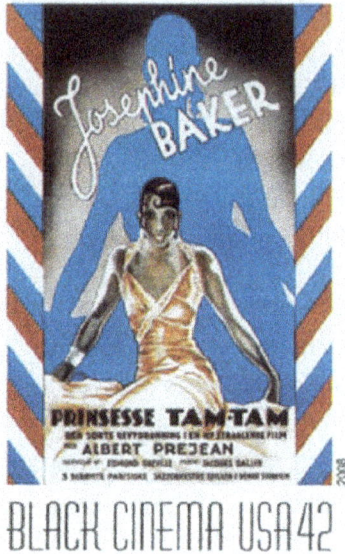

In 2008, Singer, Dancer and Actress, Josephine Baker was commemorated on the U.S. postage stamp. In 1927, she became the first African-American woman to star in a major motion picture.

"All my life, I have maintained that the people of the world can learn to live together in peace if they are not brought up in prejudice."

-- *Josephine Baker*

Woodson's continued effort on shining a light on African-American accomplishments was gaining momentum, many entertainers of the 1920's and 1930's began using their career as a platform to create change in the world. As a world renowned entertainer and singer, Josephine Baker was a trailblazer and social campaigner who fought against racial injustice throughout her career.

As an American woman she moved to France and became a French citizen, she symbolized the beauty and vitality of African-American culture when she took Paris by storm in the 1920's. She also became the first African-American woman to star in a major motion picture, which was the 1927 film "Siren of the Tropics."

During World War II, the German Army invaded France, and Baker joined the fight against the Nazi regime. She aided French military officials by passing on secrets she heard while performing in front of the enemy. She transported the confidential information by writing with invisible ink on music sheets. When the war ended, she became the first American woman ever to receive French military honors.

Baker returned home to the U.S. and became involved with the civil rights movement and worked closely with the National Association for the Advancement of Colored People (NAACP). In 1963, she was one of a few women who spoke at the March on Washington for Jobs and Freedom alongside Dr. Martin Luther King Jr. and other civil rights leaders.

Her speech detailed her life and experience as an African-American woman in the United States and abroad in Europe. In recognition of her opposition to social injustice, and work as a staunch civil rights activist, the NAACP declared May 20th as "Josephine Baker Day" in her honor.

As her reputation grew as a crusader, she refused to perform for segregated audiences in the United States. Her insistence helped to integrate live entertainment shows across the country, including the cities of Miami, Chicago and Las Vegas.

In 1990 and 1995, Track and Field star, Jesse Owens was commemorated on the U.S. postage stamp. In 1936, he achieved international fame by winning four gold medals as well as breaking two Olympic records at the Summer Olympics in Berlin, Germany.

"We all have dreams, but in order to make our dreams come into reality, it takes an awful lot of determination, dedication, self discipline and effort."

-- Jesse Owens

Ten years after establishing Negro History Week as an annual celebration, with the commemoration being the second week of February, Woodson noticed many African-American athletes were beginning to emerge as national heroes and seen as larger than life.

In 1936, Track and Field athlete, Jesse Owens achieved international fame by winning four gold medals as well as breaking two Olympic records at the Summer Olympics in Berlin, Germany. Known as "The Buckeye Bullet," Owens began his athletic career in High School when he won three Track and Field events at the 1933 National Interscholastic Championship.

Two years later while competing for Ohio State University, he equaled one world record and broke three others before qualifying and competing in the 1936 Olympics. He was the most successful athlete at the games and as an African-American man, he was credited with "single-handedly crushing the Nazi myth of Aryan supremacy." In all, the United States won eleven gold medals, six of them by African-American athletes. Owens was easily the most dominant athlete to compete.

Although the Olympic games in 1936 were hosted by Nazi Germany, thousands of fans adored Owens as he arrived at the new Olympic stadium, many of the young women shouted "Where is Jesse? Where is Jesse?" Despite the politically charged atmosphere of the Berlin Games, Owens was adored by the German public, he won three individual gold medals and a fourth as a member of the triumphant U.S. 4 × 100 meter relay team.

Just before the Track and Field competitions began, the founder of Adidas athletic shoe company, Adi Dassler personally visited Owens in the Olympic village and persuaded him to wear his Adidas branded shoes, this was the first time a sponsorship was offered to an African-American athlete. After returning to the United States, Owens was hailed as a national hero and greeted by New York City Mayor, Fiorello LaGuardia, a ticker-tape parade in Manhattan was given in his honor.

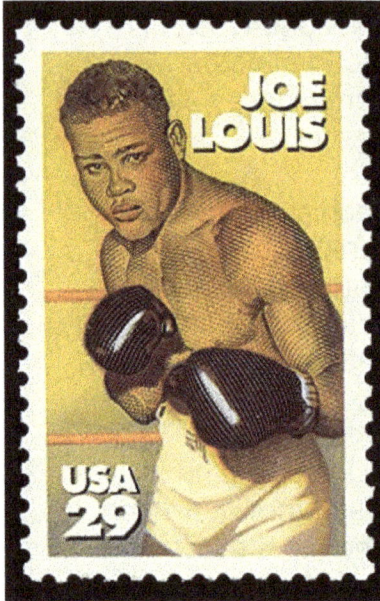

In 1993, Heavyweight Boxing Champion Joe Louis was commemorated on the U.S. postage stamp. He is regarded as one of the sport's all-time greats and considered the first true African-American national hero in the United States.

"I hope they're still making women like my momma. She always told me to do the right thing. She always told me to have pride in myself; she said a good name is better than money."

-- *Joe Louis*

In 1938, Woodson recognized another athlete who rose to prominence, who was considered the first African-American person to achieve the status of a national hero within the United States. Boxer, Joe Louis reigned as World Heavyweight Champion for over thirteen years, he is also regarded as one of the sport's all-time greats.

Louis was the focal point of African-American pride in the 1930's, his reign as champion was the longest in the history of boxing, and he successfully defended his title 25 times, more than any other champion in any division. Known as the "Brown Bomber," Louis, scored a total of 52 knockouts during his career, he was known as an extremely accurate and powerful knockout puncher.

He sustained his first professional loss in 1936 at the hands of German boxer, Max Schmeling. As Schmeling handed Louis his only defeat, their rematch was scheduled two years later in 1938 at Yankee Stadium. The fate of the world had changed considerably since their first match, and a Louis-Schmeling rematch became a prelude to World War II. As Adolf Hitler's army already began marching through Europe, what mattered most to the 80,000 fans that packed into Yankee Stadium was Schmeling's nationality, he was German, and Hitler was hailing him as proof of Aryan racial superiority.

As Louis entered the ring, he walked across the field of Yankee Stadium with the weight of his country and the world on his shoulders. This was far more than the twenty-four year old Louis had signed on for. This boxing match, with all of its political implications, soon morphed into President Roosevelt vs. Hitler, Democracy vs. Fascism, and Good vs. Evil. Nearly 100 million listeners around the world tuned in to the fight on the radio, as it was the most highly anticipated event of 1938.

Louis defeated Schmeling with a devastating first round knockout, proving Aryan supremacy does not exist, as he was instantly hailed as a national hero. The fight is regarded as the most important and historic sporting event of all time. This event was truly monumental, as it was the first time in history that Caucasian sports fans in America openly cheered for an African-American athlete against a Caucasian opponent.

In 2005, Activist and Singer, Marian Anderson was commemorated on the U.S. postage stamp. She is regarded as one as one of the most celebrated singers of the 20th century and a trailblazer in the struggle for African-American artists trying to overcome racial injustice in the United States.

"If you have a purpose in which you can believe, there's no end to the amount of things you can accomplish."

-- *Marian Anderson*

As Woodson continued his journey of educating the masses about African-American contributions, activist and singer, Marian Anderson emerged as one of the most celebrated singers of the early 20th century, she broke through many barriers for African-American artists during her career. She was a trailblazer in the struggle for African-American artists trying to overcome racial injustice in the United States.

In 1935, Anderson became the first African-American singer to perform as a member of the Metropolitan Opera in New York City, that same year, she also made her concert debut at "Town Hall" in Midtown Manhattan. Most of her singing career was spent performing in concert venues with major orchestras throughout the United States and Europe.

In 1939, she attempted to rent a concert facility in Washington, D.C.'s Constitution Hall, and was refused due to her race. The incident sparked widespread outrage and protest from many people, including First Lady Eleanor Roosevelt. Arrangements were made for Anderson to instead appear at the Lincoln Memorial on Easter Sunday in 1939. She performed a critically acclaimed open-air concert on the steps of the Lincoln Memorial and sang before an integrated crowd of more than 75,000 people, and a radio audience in the tens of millions. Her pure vocal quality, richness of tone, and tremendous range made her, in the opinion of many, the world's greatest singer.

Anderson later became an important symbol of grace and beauty during the civil rights movement in the 1960's, notably singing at the March on Washington in 1963. She also worked for several years as a delegate to the "United Nations Human Rights Committee" and as a "Goodwill Ambassadress" for the U.S. Department of State. Her voice had made her famous on both sides of the Atlantic. As a personal friend of President Franklin D. Roosevelt and First Lady Eleanor, she was often invited to perform at White House events.

In 1997, Benjamin O. Davis Sr., was commemorated on the U.S. postage stamp. In 1940, he became the first African-American to rise to the rank of General in the U.S. Army.

As World War II emerged and continued into the 1940's, there were many unsung African-American war hero's that rose through the ranks in the U.S. military. Prior to the war beginning, Benjamin Davis, Sr. already had four decades of service in the military. He enlisted as a private in the 9th Cavalry of the U.S. Army and rose to sergeant major within two years earning a commission as second lieutenant in 1901.

He served in Liberia and the Philippines while later teaching military science at Tuskegee Institute and Wilberforce University. He rose slowly through the ranks, becoming the first African-American Colonel in the U.S. Army in 1930. While serving, Davis led the fight against enemy forces both foreign and domestic. In 1940, President Franklin D. Roosevelt promoted Davis as the first African-American General in the Army.

Davis battled segregation in the military by developing and implementing plans to desegregate of U.S. combat forces in Europe during World War II. Following his many years of service, Davis became an advisor for the military on racial discrimination by pushing for full integration of Armed Forces.

Two American Navy Destroyer Ships, the USS Mason and the Submarine Chaser, PC1264, were staffed entirely by African-American crews following a letter sent to President Roosevelt by the NAACP, demanding that African-Americans be used in roles other than mess-men in the U.S. military.

The momentum of the NAACP and the African-American community forced President Roosevelt to deal with the issue of segregation against African-Americans in the Armed Services during World War II, Davis was instrumental in Rosevelt's decision to desegregate.

In 1948, after fifty years of military service, Davis retired in a public ceremony with President Harry S. Truman presiding. Six days later on July 26, 1948, President Truman issued Executive Order 9981 which abolished racial discrimination in all of the branches of the United States Armed Forces.

In 2006, Hattie McDaniel was commemorated on the U.S. postage stamp. In 1940, she became the first African-American to receive an Academy Award, she won "Best Supporting Actress" for her role in the motion picture, "Gone with the Wind."

McDaniel also has two stars on the Hollywood Walk of Fame, one for her contributions to radio, and one for acting in motion pictures.

While Woodson was persuading organizations and schools to take part in new programs in order to advocate and influence others to learn more about African-American history, there were many pioneers and trendsetters emerging in music and entertainment arenas. During the 1930's and 1940's, actress, singer and songwriter, Hattie McDaniel broke through several barriers for African-American performers.

As an actress, she appeared in over 300 motion pictures during her career. In addition to acting, she was also a radio performer and television star, she became the first African-American woman to sing on the radio in the United States. In 1934, she joined the Screen Actors Guild and began to attract attention while landing larger film roles which earned her screen credits.

In 1940, McDaniel became the first African-American to win an Academy Award, she won "Best Supporting Actress" for her role in the motion picture, "Gone with the Wind," her acceptance speech was hailed as the greatest speech ever given on the Academy floor.

McDaniel's often shared her success by uplifting peers in her community, she had an open door policy with fellow African-American performers at her L.A. home on South Harvard Street. She also donated generously to educational causes, including the National Association for the Advancement of Colored People (NAACP), and scholarships for her sorority, Sigma Gamma Rho. Woodson admired McDaniel as she used her success to improve the lives of others.

During World War II, she served as chairman of the Hollywood Victory Committee, an organization that provided entertainment for soldiers stationed at military bases throughout the country. McDaniel made numerous personal appearances at military hospitals and performed at several celebrity events in order to raise funds to support the war.

In 2014, Charles Alfred "Chief" Anderson was commemorated on the U.S. postage stamp. Known as the "Father of Black Aviation" he was the Chief Flight Instructor of the prestigious Tuskegee Airmen.

As momentum for Negro History Week continued to gather steam for the following decades as the commemoration of African-American contributions became a cultural fixture. The Tuskegee Airmen were making their own history as the first African-American military aviators in the U.S. Army Air Corps (AAC), a precursor of the U.S. Air Force.

Known as the "Father of African-American Aviation," Charles Alfred Anderson Sr. was recruited by the Tuskegee Institute as the Chief Civilian Flight Instructor for its new program to train African-American pilots. He developed the military training program and taught hundreds of pilots how to fly and navigate their aircraft, earning his nickname, "The Chief."

President Roosevelt's administration explored the possibility of training African-American pilots for military service. In 1941, First Lady Eleanor Roosevelt toured the Institute's hospital. Knowing of the flight program, she asked to meet its chief instructor and asked Anderson for a flight, it was a great experience for both as the flight lasted 40 minutes.

Anderson was then selected by the Army as Tuskegee's Ground Commander and Chief Instructor for aviation cadets of the 99th Pursuit Squadron, America's first African-American fighter squadron, which later included two other squadrons of Tuskegee Airmen, the 332nd Fighter Group and the "Red Tails."

They were deemed the first African-American war heroes during World War II, as they destroyed 260 German planes, thousands of rail cars, transport vehicles and a German destroyer.

As they flew more than 15,000 individual missions over two years, the Tuskegee Airmen never lost a bomber in more than 200 escorts. Their group of distinguished airmen represented an important step forward in preparing the nation for the racial integration of the U.S. Military. A number of Tuskegee Airmen later received purple hearts and congressional medals of honors for their bravery and service.

In 2000, Jackie Robinson was commemorated on the U.S. postage stamp. Throughout his career, he was the recipient of the Inaugural Major League Baseball (MLB) Rookie of the Year Award in 1947, an All-Star for six consecutive seasons from 1949 through 1954, he also won the National League Most Valuable Player (MVP) Award in 1949. Robinson played in six World Series and contributed to the Dodgers 1955 World Series Championship.

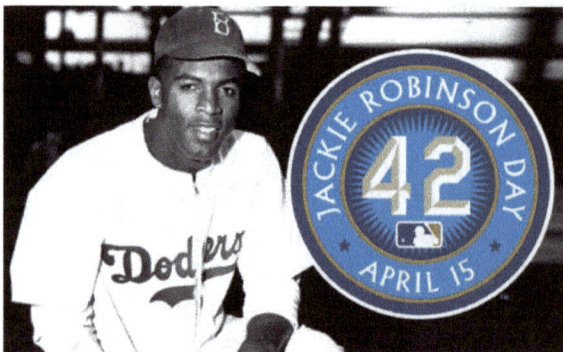

"Life is not a spectator sport. If you're going to spend your whole life in the grandstand just watching what goes on, in my opinion you're wasting your life."

-- *Jackie Robinson*

As professional baseball was the most popular and dominant sport in the United States during the early 1940's, Jackie Robinson became the first African-American to play Major League Baseball, he broke the color barrier in 1947 and debuted with the Brooklyn Dodgers as a "Third- Baseman." He played his historic first game against the Boston Braves at Ebbetts Field in Brooklyn on April 15, 1947.

Prior to playing professional baseball he served as a second lieutenant in the United States Army from 1942 to 1944. During boot camp in Fort Hood, TX, Robinson was arrested and court-martialed in 1944 for refusing to give up his seat and move to the back of a segregated bus. Along with his excellent reputation as a soldier, combined with the efforts of his community, the NAACP and various African-American owned newspapers in the country were able to shed public light on the injustice.

Ultimately he was acquitted of the charges and received an honorable discharge. His courage and moral objection to racial segregation were precursors to the impact Robinson had in Major League Baseball. He began his professional baseball career as he succeeded in putting the prejudice and racism he encountered aside and showed everyone what a talented player he was. Robinson was named Rookie of the Year as he batted .297 with 12 home runs and helped the Dodgers win the National League pennant.

The impact Robinson made on Major League Baseball is one that will be remembered forever. On April 15th each season, every team in the Major League celebrates "Jackie Robinson Day" in honor of when he truly broke the color barrier in baseball, becoming the first African-American player in the 20th century to take the field in the Majors.

Robinson was a vocal champion for African-American athletes and other social and political causes. In 1949, he testified about discrimination before the House Un-American Activities Committee, he also served on the board of the NAACP until 1967. After his retirement from baseball, he continued to lobby for greater racial integration in all sports.

In 2017, Dorothy Height was commemorated on the U.S. postage stamp. She is credited as the first leader in the civil rights movement to recognize inequality for women. She was the president of the National Council of Negro Women for forty years.

"Greatness is not measured by what a man or woman accomplishes, but by the opposition he or she has overcome to reach his goals."

-- *Dorothy Height*

Chapter 9 - Emerging Hero's of a New Movement

Along with the annual observance of Negro History Week and his publications becoming more popular, Woodson began witnessing a new generation of African-American dreamers, innovators and record breakers who were symbols of pride and aspirations during the 1940's and 1950's. As World War II ended the United States was preceded by decades of campaigns by African-Americans and their allies to end legalized racial discrimination, disenfranchisement and racial segregation in America.

These events helped set the stage for grass-roots initiatives to enact racial equality legislation and incite a civil rights movement. In 1937, Dorothy Height met her hero and future mentor, Mary McLeod Bethune, Founder and President of the National Council of Negro Women (NCNW). Bethune appointed Height as the new President of the NCNW, a position she would hold for forty-one years. Height led the NCNW during the civil rights era of the 1950's and 1960's.

Under her leadership, the NCNW supported voter registration in the South and financially aided several civil rights activists throughout the country. Height's prominence in the civil rights movement and unmatched knowledge in organizing, meant she was regularly called to give advice on political issues. First Lady Eleanor Roosevelt along with Presidents, Franklin D Rosevelt, Dwight D. Eisenhower, and Lyndon B. Johnson often sought her counsel.

As President, she helped to organize "The March on Washington" in 1963. She has worked with every major civil rights leader of the period, including Dr. Martin Luther King, Jr., Roy Wilkins, Whitney Young, and A. Philip Randolph. She also personally encouraged President Dwight Eisenhower to desegregate public schools and urged President Lyndon B. Johnson to appoint African-American women into governmental positions.

In 1998, Mahalia Jackson was commemorated on the U.S. postage stamp. Known as "The Queen of Gospel," she is revered as one of the greatest musical figures in U.S. History.

"If you believe in God, He will open the windows of heaven and pour blessings upon you."

-- Mahalia Jackson

As Carter G. Woodson devoted most of his life to preserving the history of African-Americans, his efforts succeeded as Negro History Week entered a new decade. In 1950, Woodson passed away at his home in Washington D.C. at the age of seventy-four. It was apparent that the organization he started, the Association for the Study of African-American Life and History (ASALH) continued through successive generations that made African-American studies a staple of most American institutes of higher learning, as a new generation continued making their own history.

During the 1950's, the church served as a staple in African-American communities across America. Gospel music was used to express faith in the Lord, and also used while marching to protest injustice and segregation. Known as "The Queen of Gospel," singer, Mahalia Jackson is revered as one of the greatest musical figures in U.S. history. She became one of Gospel music's all-time greats, as she was known for her powerful voice that cultivated a global following.

Jackson was a staunch supporter of the civil rights movement which began in the 1950's. She sang at the March on Washington in 1963 at the request of her friend, Dr. Martin Luther King, Jr. She sang the songs "How I Got Over" and "I Been Buked and I Been Scorned" in front of a crowd of 250,000 people. Motivated by her sincere appreciation that most civil rights protests were being organized within churches and its participants were inspired by hymns, she also traveled to Montgomery, Alabama to sing in support of the ongoing bus boycott in 1955.

Jackson prompted Dr. King to improvise his "I Have a Dream" speech. Recalling a theme she heard him use in one of his earlier speeches, she said out loud to Dr. King, as he was behind the podium on the steps of the Lincoln Memorial, "Tell them about the dream, Martin," with her advice, he placed his prepared notes away and went on to deliver one of the greatest speeches in U.S. history. As a world renown figure, her gift of music brought people of different religious and political convictions together to revel in the beauty of the Gospels and to appreciate the warm spirit that underscored the way she lived her life.

In 2003, Thurgood Marshall was commemorated on the U.S. postage stamp. He served as the first African-American Supreme Court Justice in the United States.

"A man can make what he wants of himself if he truly believes that he must be ready for hard work and many heartbreaks."

-- *Thurgood Marshall*

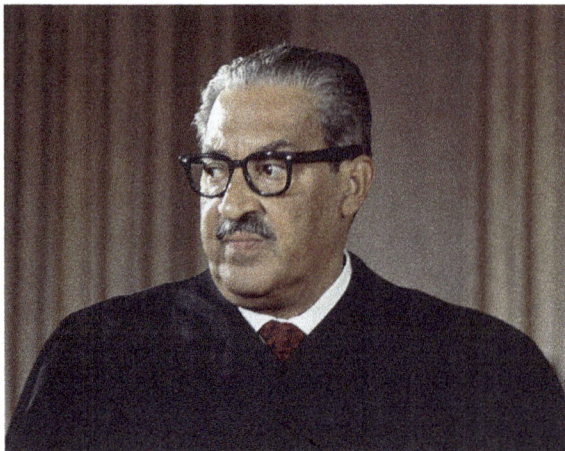

The civil rights movement was a struggle for social justice that took place mainly during the 1950's and 1960's for African-Americans to gain equal rights under the law in the United States. The civil war officially abolished slavery, but it didn't end discrimination against African-American people living in America. As they mobilized and began an unprecedented fight for freedom and equality, many new leaders emerged including Thurgood Marshall, who was the chief attorney of the NAACP Legal Defense Fund for twenty-three years.

During his tenure with the NAACP, he distinguished himself for using the legal system to break racially discriminatory practices in voting, housing, transportation as well as education. Marshall succeeded in having the Supreme Court declare segregated public schools as unconstitutional. The 1954 landmark case Brown vs. Board of Education was one of the cornerstones of the civil rights movement, it helped to establish the precedent that "separate-but-equal" education and other services were not, in fact, equal at all.

Marshall played an instrumental role in promoting racial equality during the civil rights movement. As a practicing attorney, he argued a record-breaking 32 cases before the Supreme Court, winning 29 of them. He represented and won more cases before the high court than any other person in history.

His passion for ensuring the rights of all citizens regardless of race caught the attention of President John F. Kennedy, who appointed him to the U.S. court of appeals. In 1965, President Lyndon B. Johnson appointed Marshall to the post of Solicitor General (this person argues cases on behalf of the U.S. Government before the Supreme Court, it is the third highest office in the Justice Department).

In 1967, President Johnson then appointed Marshall as the first African-American U.S. Supreme Court Justice. Throughout his historic tenure as a Supreme Court Justice, Marshall developed a reputation as a passionate member of the court who supported expanding civil rights, his passionate support for individual and civil rights guided his policies and decisions.

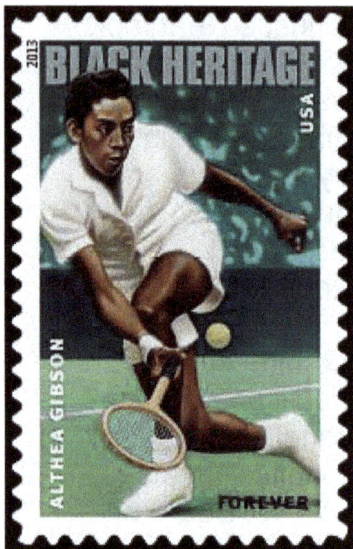

In 2013, Tennis and Golf star Althea Gibson was commemorated on the U.S. postage stamp. Gibson broke the color barrier in both sports and became the first African-American to compete and win major tennis titles at the French Open, the U.S. Open and Wimbledon competitions.

"I always wanted to be somebody. If I made it, it's half because I was game enough to take a lot of punishment along the way, and half because there were a lot of people who cared enough to help me."

-- *Althea Gibson*

72

As Jackie Robinson became an iconic symbol in the United States as the man who broke the color barrier in sports, Althea Gibson became a major figure in her own right as she was the first international sports star of the 1950's. As the first African-American to compete in a national championship for tennis, she became a trailblazer in the sports world, overcoming racial blockades that would change the game for succeeding generations.

Gibson's career began in the height of the civil rights movement. As she competed for a tennis championship on a world stage, her athletic talents helped to uplift the movement and African-American pride nationwide, she was also the first American woman to appear on the cover of Time Magazine and Sports Illustrated.

In 1956, Gibson became the first African-American to win a major tennis title when she won the women's singles in the French Open. She made history once again in 1957, as she became the first African-American player to compete and win at the U.S. Open and Wimbledon, an international tennis championship.

While dominating the women's portion, winning both the singles and doubles championships, she became the first champion ever to receive their trophy personally presented to them from royalty, as she shook hands with Queen Elizabeth II.

After Gibson was named the Female Athlete of the Year by the Associated Press two years in a row in 1957 and 1958, she became a professional tennis player in 1959, winning a total of fifty-six singles and doubles championship matches, and collected eleven grand slam titles, including six doubles titles.

Known as one of the "greatest tennis players who ever lived," Gibson was later inducted into the International Tennis Hall of Fame and the International Women's Sports Hall of Fame. Establishing herself as a legend in tennis, Gibson also broke the color barrier in the sport of golf, she became the first African-American golfer in the Ladies Professional Golf Association (LPGA). As a golfer, she competed in 171 events between 1963 and 1977 on the women's professional golf tour.

"Being the Queen is not all about singing, and being a Diva is not all about singing. It has much to do with your service to people. And your social contributions to your community and your civic contributions as well."

-- *Aretha Franklin*

During the civil rights movement, African-American artists have traditionally been agents of change through their music, reflecting and shaping the issues of the time. Whether it was the voice of suffering in Billie Holliday's "Strange Fruit," the passion of Nina Simone's "How It Would Feel To Be Free," or the funky soul of James Brown's "Say It Loud - I'm Black and I'm Proud," these musicians had a massive impact of the movement.

As a daughter of the movement, soul singer, Aretha Franklin was a voice of pride, hope and freedom. Her rendition of the Otis Redding song "Respect" became an anthem of empowerment for African-Americans as well as all women in the country. Franklin's advocacy for the African-American community was undeniable.

During the 1960's, she was considered a symbol of African-American pride through her music. She not only used her voice to entertain, but also to uplift and inspire generations through her songs. Her singles "You Make Me Feel Like a Natural Woman," "Young, Gifted, and Black," and "Think" became anthems reflecting the country's growing concerns over racial injustice.

Known as the "Queen of Soul, her iconic performances and productions came to define the term "soul music" in the 20th century, setting the standard for African-American female vocal excellence.

Franklin's activist roots came from her father, Reverend C.L. Franklin, an organizer and close personal friend of Dr. Martin Luther King Jr. His 1963 Detroit Walk to Freedom predated King's March on Washington by two months, which set the stage for America's then-largest civil rights demonstration.

Her family's ties to the movement were born from her father's relationships with prominent activists of the 1960's, such as Dr. King, Mahalia Jackson, and Harry Belafonte. Franklin remained a prominent face and voice for civil rights, her commitment to equality changed many hearts and minds during the movement. Franklin took Soul music to unprecedented heights as she became the first woman to be inducted into the Rock & Roll Hall of Fame in 1987.

In 1999, Dr. Martin Luther King Jr. was commemorated on the U.S. postage stamp. As a civil rights leader, he was a staunch believer in exclusively nonviolent protest. Dr. King is the first African-American honored with a memorial on the National Mall in Washington D.C.

"We know through painful experience that freedom is never voluntarily given by the oppressor; it must be demanded by the oppressed."

-- *Dr. Martin Luther King Jr.*

Throughout the 1950's and the 1960's, Dr. Martin Luther King Jr. also played a key role in the civil rights movement. He sought equality and human rights for African-Americans, the economically disadvantaged, and all victims of injustice through peaceful protest. He is best known for his role in the advancement of civil rights using the tactics of nonviolence and civil disobedience based on his Christian beliefs as well as being inspired by the nonviolent activism of Mahatma Gandhi.

In 1963, "The March on Washington for Jobs and Freedom" was held in Washington, D.C. The purpose of the march was to advocate for civil and economic rights for African-Americans. Dr. King stood in front of the Lincoln Memorial and delivered his historic "I Have a Dream" speech, which he called for an end to racism and injustice. This was a peaceful demonstration to focus national attention on equality for African-Americans as well as advance the civil rights bill that was before Congress.

In 1964, the civil rights movement achieved two of its greatest successes, the ratification of the 24th Amendment, which abolished the poll tax, and the civil rights act of 1964, which prohibited racial discrimination in employment, education, and outlawed racial segregation in public facilities. In 1964, Dr. King also became the youngest African-American to be awarded the Nobel Peace Prize, he donated the prize money, valued at $54,600 to the civil rights movement.

In 1965, King's elevated profile drew international attention to the violence that erupted between segregationists and peaceful demonstrators in Selma, Alabama, where the Southern Christian Leadership Conference (SCLC) and Student Nonviolent Coordinating Committee (SNCC) organized a voter registration campaign.

Dr. King then lead a 54 mile march from Selma to Montgomery, AL. The initial 3,300 marchers at the beginning, eventually grew to 50,000 when they reached the Alabama Capitol. After the march, President Lyndon B. Johnson proposed the "Voting Rights Act," which secured the right to vote for minorities throughout the country.

NASA Mathematicians, Katherine Johnson, Dorothy Vaughan and Mary Jackson all played a critical role in providing data that was essential to the success of the early U.S. Space Program in the 1960's.

In 1961, following the successful Russian Satellite Launch, there was pressure on America to send their own into space. Three brilliant African-American women at NASA, Katherine Johnson, Dorothy Vaughan and Mary Jackson served as the brains behind one of the greatest operations in U.S. history, the launch of Astronaut, John Glenn into orbit. A stunning achievement that restored the Nation's confidence, turned around the "Space Race" and galvanized the world.

Johnson, Vaughan and Jackson, shattered the segregational norms within the agency in the 1960's to push forward some of the country's greatest aerospace advancements. Known as "Hidden Figures" they joined dozens of other African-American women who crunched numbers and processed data for the National Advisory Committee for Aeronautics (NACA) and its successor, the National Aeronautics and Space Administration (NASA). As many of these women began their career, they were referred to as "human computers," as they performed complicated calculations that supported the work of male engineers.

Although African-American women faced barriers due to racial discrimination, they played a critical role in providing data that was essential to the success of the early U.S. space program. They rose to new heights as mathematicians, computer programmers, team project leads, and engineers at NASA. Johnson analyzed the flight trajectory and verified computer calculations for space travel missions, her math also helped Project Apollo to send astronauts to the moon, while also making future moon landings a reality.

Vaughan worked with leading computer operators and engineers, becoming an expert in coding language at NASA, she also worked on the "Launch Vehicle Program" that sent satellites into space. As a research mathematician, Jackson analyzed data from wind tunnel experiments and real-world aircraft flight experiments which included thrust and drag forces. All three women helped broaden the scope for space travel, chartering new frontiers for humanities exploration of space and creating new possibilities for all human kind. They all played a major role in many of NASA's important milestones.

In 2018, Singer, Actress and Civil Rights Activist, Lena Horne was commemorated on the U.S. postage stamp. As a leader in civil rights movement, she also spoke out against social injustice and raised money for various civil rights causes. Her legendary career as a recording artist which spanned over seven decades brought her immense popularity and acclaim.

"I'm me, and I'm like nobody else."

-- Lena Horne

During the 1960's, the fight for equal rights was also at its height in the entertainment industry. As a singer and actress, Lena Horne championed for racial and social justice during her entire career. She entered show business at the age of sixteen, and in 1942, she became the first African-American performer to sign a long-term contract with a major Hollywood studio, Metro Goldwyn Mayer (MGM). She insisted on not being relegated to roles where she would play a domestic worker, which was the industry standard for African-American screen performers at the time.

Horne also continued to fight racial and social injustices throughout her career, fundraising for groups like the NAACP and the National Council of Negro Women, and singing at civil rights rallies, including the March on Washington protest in 1963.

Horne revolutionized the entertainment industry as she was one of the most recognizable actors, singers and civil rights icons of her era. Her success as an actress was also recognized when she became a member of the board of the Screen Actors Guild.

Several of Horne's roles in motion pictures were similar, her image was always elegantly gowned, singing while draped around a marble column in a lavishly produced musical sequence, this would become virtually standardized.

Her legendary career as a recording artist which spanned over an unprecedented seven decades also brought her immense popularity and acclaim. Her fight against discrimination helped break barriers, challenge stereotypes and pave the way for more African-American women to find their own place in the industry.

As a civil rights pioneer, Horne was admired around the world, not only for her talent, but for her integrity and activism. She often used her platform to speak out, as she refused to perform for segregated audiences. Although Horne has enjoyed lasting success as a performer, some observers consider her most important role as a trailblazer, who elevated the status of African-Americans in the performing arts.

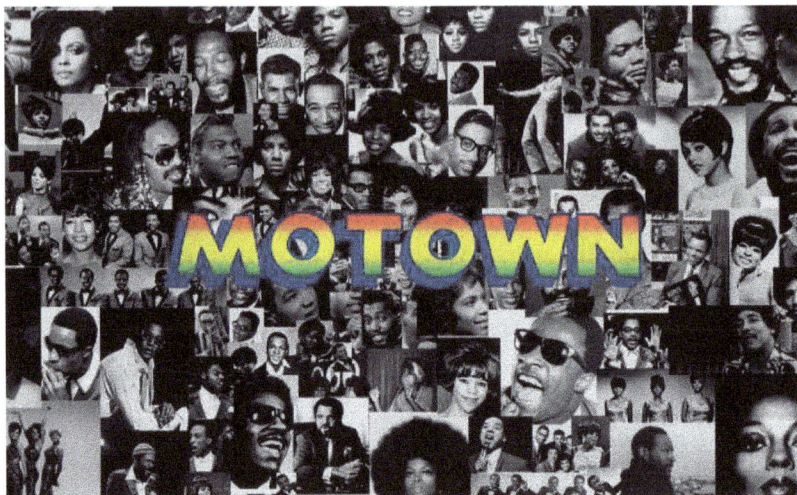

"*Motown was about music for all people, I was reluctant to have our music alienate anyone.*"

-- *Berry Gordy*

As the civil rights movement continued during the 1960's, a new soulful sound that changed the history of American music forever was born in Detroit, MI. Founded by songwriter, Berry Gordy in 1959, Motown Records played an important role in the racial integration of popular music. As an African-American owned record label, it achieved crossover success while crafting Americas soundtrack.

As the founder of Motown Records, Berry Gordy is responsible for creating the hit-making enterprise that nurtured the careers of countless musical legends including Diana Ross, Marvin Gaye, Stevie Wonder, The Temptations, Michael Jackson, Smokey Robinson, and many others among its hundreds of signings.

As a record company and label, Motown created a new soulful sound that had an enduring power, while creating a bond that echoed throughout the world. The "Motown Sound" reached out across a racial divide, while politically and socially transforming popular music. Despite the hostility and racism throughout the country during the time, the "Motown Sound" would often bring people together through soul and pop music.

As Motown artists began touring the country, concert audiences were often segregated during their performances. People who often couldn't find anything in common with each other were starting to finally come together with their love of music. The Motown sound had the power to make people forget their differences and come together and sing and dance. As a thirty year old executive, Gordy was a true visionary, his record label and artists forever transformed the landscape of soul and pop music forever, as it evolved into the new "Sound of Young America."

During the late 1960's, songs of freedom began to rang out loud during the civil rights movement, Motown artists began writing more socially conscious music that motivated and inspired people who were fighting for equal rights and justice. Songs like "What's Going On?" by Marvin Gaye became an anthem that addressed an entire generation of growing skepticism of the Vietnam War, and a desire to do away with social inequalities in the United States and abroad.

"Impossible is just a big word thrown around by small men who find it easier to live in the world they've been given than to explore the power they have to change it. Impossible is not a fact, it's an opinion. Impossible is not a declaration, it's a dare. Impossible is potential. Impossible is temporary. Impossible is nothing."

-- Muhammad Ali

The 1960's also introduced an eighteen year old boxer named Cassius Clay, who won a gold medal on the U.S. Olympic boxing team in Rome, Italy. At 6-foot-3-inches tall, Clay made boxing an art with his lightening speed and fancy footwork. He was just as fast with his words as he was with his jabs and his feet. Upon returning home as a gold medalist, he emerged as a civil rights activist and contender for the heavyweight title. In 1964, he shocked the world as he defeated the undefeated heavyweight champion Sonny Liston in a 7th round knock out.

Prior to his win against Liston, Clay attended several Nation of Islam meetings. After the fight, he surprised the world when he announced he accepted the teachings of Islam under Elijah Muhammad and the Minister Malcolm X influence. He denounced the name Cassius Clay, and became known as Muhammad Ali.

Ali shocked the world once again in 1967, when he refused to report to duty after being drafted into the U.S. military, citing his religious beliefs and opposition to American involvement in the Vietnam War. He also pointed out that African-American men were disproportionally drafted and killed in Vietnam, while those who returned after fighting heroically still faced racism and oppression in their own country.

Although, some were critical of his actions, the overwhelming majority felt Ali was a man of profound conviction. He had the support of many high-profile African-American athletes as well as other civil rights leaders. Although, Dr. Martin Luther King Jr. had different views than the Nation of Islam, he admired Ali's bravery and defiance, as he was a man who was willing to have his boxing title stripped away and suffer the consequences by not going to war, but instead stand up for his religious principles and his people.

Ali is regarded as one of the most significant and celebrated sports figures of the 20th century, as he is still the most recognizable person on planet earth. Known as the "Greatest of All Time," he used his platform as a world renown championship boxer to advocate for civil rights as he tried to make the world a better place for all people.

In 2014, Congresswoman Shirley Chisholm was commemorated on the U.S. postage stamp. In 1968, she became the first African-American woman elected to the United States Congress. Chisholm also became the first African-American candidate for a major party's nomination for President of the United States.

"If they don't give you a seat at the table, bring a folding chair."

-- *Shirley Chisholm*

As the civil rights movement entered a new decade, racial and gender equality were major issues that reached the national stage during the early 1970's. As the Voting Rights Act of 1965 was a landmark piece of federal legislation in the United States that prohibited racial discrimination in voting, more African-American men and woman entered local and national races for political offices.

Growing up in Brooklyn, N.Y., Shirley Chisholm was exposed to a great deal of activism, she began to pay close attention to the social issues that affected her generation. Chisholm drew upon her experiences in Brooklyn's political scene to successfully run for the New York State Assembly in 1964.

Some of her major achievements included granting domestic workers unemployment benefits and a program that awarded underprivileged students an opportunity to attend college. After four years, Chisholm ran for the seat in New York's 12th congressional district in 1968 and won, becoming the first African-American woman elected to the U.S. House of Representatives.

As an active Congresswoman in the House, Chisholm served on various committees, including the House Agriculture Committee, the Veterans Affairs Committee, and the Education Committee. She also became a co-founder the National Organization for Women (NOW) in 1970, and one of the founding members of the Congressional Black Caucus in 1971.

During her second term in Congress, Chisholm then launched her 1972 bid for presidency of the United States, making her the first African-American person to seek the presidential nomination from one of the two major political parties.

Her quest for the 1972 Democratic Party presidential nomination entered 12 primaries and garnered 152 of the delegate votes, despite having an under-financed campaign. Chisholm's campaign shook up the political world as she pushed a platform that focused on racial and gender equality, elevating those issues to a national stage.

Close to fifty years after Carter G. Woodson started Negro History Week in 1926, a student organization named "Black United Students" on the campus of Kent State University proposed the first ever month-long celebration of Black History at the university in 1969. The following year, the first ever celebration of Black History Month took place on the campus in February, 1970.

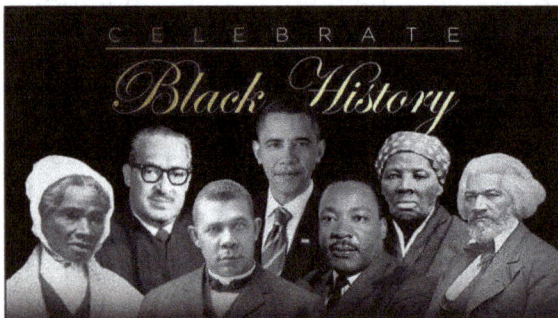

Chapter 10 - Observance for Black History Month Begins

For close to five decades after educator and historian, Carter G. Woodson and his organization, the Association for the Study of African-American Life and History (ASALH) announced the second week of February as Negro History Week in 1926, there was tremendous momentum and progress to continue his journey of educating the masses about African-American contributions to the world.

In 1969, a student organization named "Black United Students" on the campus of Kent State University proposed the first ever month-long celebration of Black History at the university. The following year, the first ever celebration of Black History Month took place on the campus in February, 1970. The celebration was a reflection of African-American events and individual accomplishments throughout history.

Along with Kent State's annual celebration becoming increasingly popular each year, and the civil rights movement producing several iconic hero's, a growing awareness of African-American pride and identity soon evolved into Black History Month celebrations on many other college campuses across the country each year.

Fifty years after the first celebration, Black History Month was expanded to a month in 1976, in conjunction with the Bicentennial Celebration. President Gerald R. Ford urged Americans to "seize the opportunity to honor the too-often neglected accomplishments of African-Americans in every area of endeavor throughout our history." By this time, the entire nation had come to recognize the importance of African-American history and how it was a major part of the American story. Since then, each American president has issued Black History Month proclamations in the month of February.

In 1976, author, Alex Haley published the novel "Roots: The Saga of an American Family," which was based on his family's history, going back to the 18th century.
His novel began with the story of Kunta Kinte, who was kidnapped from Gambia, West Africa in 1767, and transported to the Province of Maryland in the U.S. and sold into slavey.

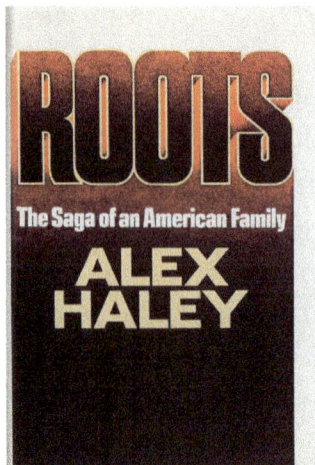

"In every conceivable manner, the family is link to our past, bridge to our future."

-- *Alex Haley*

As Black History Month was established as an annual observance throughout the month of February in the United States, soon after, the United Kingdom, the Netherlands, Canada, and the Republic of Ireland also began establishing an annual observance as well. These countries also celebrated and highlighted individuals of the African Diaspora and their contributions to the world.

During the mid 1970's, African-Americans were becoming more intrigued about their heritage tracing back to the continent of Africa. In 1976, author, Alex Haley published the novel, "Roots: The Saga of an American Family," which was based on his family's history, going back to the 18th century.

His novel began with the story of Kunta Kinte, who was kidnapped from Gambia, West Africa in 1767, and transported to the Province of Maryland in the U.S. and sold into slavery.

Haley claimed to be a seventh-generation descendant of Kinte, and his work on the novel involved twelve years of research, intercontinental travel, and writing. He visited the village of Juffure, where Kinte grew up, he listened to a tribal historian (griot) tell the story of Kinte's capture. Haley also traced the records of the ship, "The Lord Ligonier," which transported his ancestor to America.

Haley became the first African-American to win a "Special Pulitzer Prize" for his publication. In 1977, Roots was then adapted as a popular television miniseries of the same name on the ABC Network. The television series "Roots" became the most-watched dramatic show in television history, it was aired as an eight-episode miniseries and 130 million viewers tuned in.

Roots became so popular, it received thirty-seven Primetime Emmy Award nominations and won nine. The series also received an unprecedented Nielsen ratings for the finale, which still holds a record as the third highest rated episode for any type of television series, and the second most watched overall series finale in U.S. television history.

In 1971, Dr. Henry T. Sampson invented and patented the "Gamma-Electric Cell," a direct-conversion energy device that converts the energy generated from gamma rays into electricity. His revolutionary invention made it possible for cell phone technology to exist.

Chapter 11 - A New Generation of Innovators & Record Breakers

Black History Month began to gain more momentum throughout the 1970's and 1980's, as a new generation of African-American innovators began to emerge due to the progress made from the civil rights movement and the ongoing fight for equal rights in America. During this time, research chemical engineer and inventor, Dr. Henry T. Sampson became the first African-American to earn a PhD in Nuclear Engineering in the United States.

Sampson was a true pioneer in the field, following his graduate studies, he joined the Aerospace Corporation in El Segundo, California in 1967. As the director of planning and operations for the Space Test Program, he led senior engineering staff in every phase from planning to launching space operation of several satellites. He was a vanguard engineer who examined how to power satellites.

In 1971, Sampson invented and patented the "Gamma-Electric Cell," a direct-conversion energy device that converts the energy generated from gamma rays into electricity. His revolutionary creation made it possible for cell phone technology to exist. On April 3, 1973, the first ever cell phone call was placed in Midtown Manhattan, New York City. His new gamma-electric cell technology was used during the call.

The cell phone call was placed on a Motorola DynaTAC 8000x, a device that weighed 2.5 pounds, which is much heavier compared to the average 3 ounce cellular telephones which are used today. The prototype offered a talk time of approximately 20 minutes and it took an average of 10 hours to recharge.

Ever since that first phone call was placed, the cellular telephone has evolved into a global phenomenon. As a pioneer, Sampson improved the lives of countless people across the globe. There are currently more active mobile devices in the world than there are people. There are an estimated seventy-five billion cell phone calls made each day worldwide.

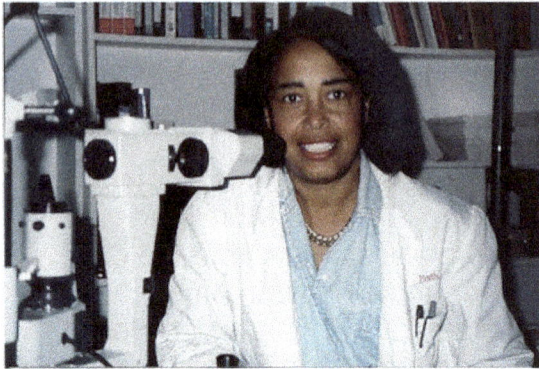

In 1981, Dr. Patricia Bath invented the Laserphaco Probe, a medical tool that is used by doctors during eye surgery to correct cataracts. Her laser device has helped restore and improve vision for millions of people worldwide.

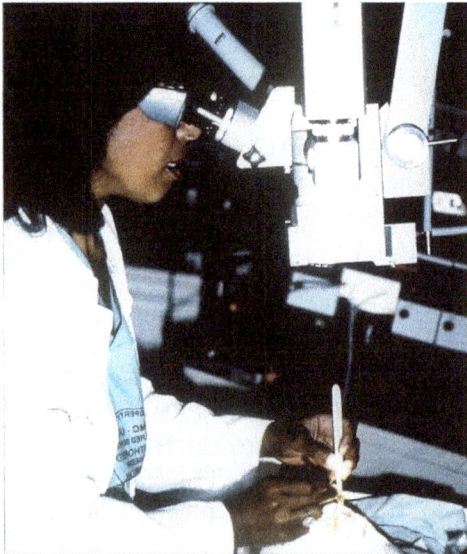

"Believe in the power of truth, do not allow your mind to be imprisoned by majority thinking, remember that the limits of science are not the limits of imagination."

-- Dr. Patricia Bath

94

During the early 1980's there were many "firsts" for African-American women, who were often changing the world with their ideas and innovation. In 1981, scientist and ophthalmologist, Dr. Patricia Bath had a passion to end blindness worldwide, as she felt eyesight was a basic human right that everyone deserved to have.

Bath was a trailblazer for women in the medical profession, she became the first African-American female doctor to secure a medical patent when she invented a surgical tool called the Laserphaco Probe. This device is a medical tool that is used when doctors perform an eye surgery on patients with cataracts, which is a cloudiness that forms in the lens of an eye, causing blurry or distorted vision, and even blindness.

Bath envisioned a way to make the surgery faster, easier, more accurate, and less invasive, her concept was more advanced than the technology used during traditional surgeries during the time. Her Laserphaco instrument consisted of a much smaller incision by using lasers, and an artificial lens can then be inserted on the eye.

Along with her groundbreaking invention, Bath along with three of her colleagues founded the American Institute for the Prevention of Blindness (AIPB), an organization whose mission is to protect, preserve, and restore the gift of eye sight. Bath along with the other founders funded the organizations largely through their own contributions and donations of equipment solicited from manufacturers.

The AIPB is based on the principle that eyesight is a basic human right, and primary eye care must be made available to all people everywhere, regardless of their economic status. As a humanitarian, Bath felt the ability to restore someones vision is the ultimate reward, during a mission in North Africa, she was able to restore the sight of a woman who had been previously blind for thirty years, as she implanted an artificial cornea during a surgical procedure.

Bath's Laserphaco has become the standard medical tool for eye surgeries in many countries around the world. She has also secured medical patents in Japan, Canada, and five European countries.

Music Conductor, Producer, Arranger, Film Composer, Television Producer, and Trumpeter, Quincy Jones is one of the most iconic music producers of the 20th century. He has dominated the entertainment industry for over six decades earning a staggering 80 Grammy Award nominations.

"Jazz has the power to make men forget their differences and come together. Jazz is the personification of transforming overwhelmingly negative circumstances into freedom, friendship, hope, and dignity."

-- Quincy Jones

During the civil rights movement, music played an important role as musicians collaborated with activists and created songs that motivated and inspired the people who were fighting for equal rights and justice. As Black History Month continued to gather steam into the 1980's, music producer, arranger, and film composer, Quincy Jones was recognized as one of the most iconic music producers of the 20th century.

His music career has led him to work on various projects with several hundred iconic African-American musicians throughout his career. During the civil rights movement, Jones worked as a social activist, supporting such programs as Dr. Martin Luther King, Jr.'s "Operation Breadbasket" in Chicago. He also joined the board of Rev. Jesse Jackson's "People United to Save Humanity" (PUSH) organization.

An ongoing concern throughout his career has been to foster appreciation of African-American music and culture, he helped to establish IBAM (Institute for Black American Music). Proceeds from IBAM events were donated toward the establishment of a national library of African-American art and music. He is also one of the founders of the annual Black Arts Festival in Chicago.

Jones has dominated the entertainment industry for over six decades, his work encompassed virtually all forms of popular music, earning him a staggering 80 Grammy Award nominations.

He is one of the most successful producers in the history of music, television and film entertainment. As the first African-American composer to be embraced by the Hollywood establishment in the 1960's, he helped refresh music in motion pictures with infusions of Jazz and Soul.

Jones was the first African-American to be nominated for an Academy Award for two categories, including, "Best Original Song" and "Best Original Score" for his work on the music for the 1967 motion picture "In Cold Blood." He has also been named as one of the most influential Jazz musicians of the 20th century.

In 1992, Engineer, Physician and NASA Astronaut, Mae C. Jemison became the first African-American woman to travel into space.

"Never be limited by other people's limited imaginations. If you adopt their attitudes, then the possibility won't exist because you'll have already shut it out. You can hear other people's wisdom, but you've got to re-evaluate the world for yourself."

-- *Mae C. Jemison*

During the 1970's and 1980's, more African-American astronauts were being recognized for their contributions to the National Aeronautics and Space Administration (NASA). While applying for admission to NASA's astronaut training program, a variety of their backgrounds included military pilots, engineers, scientists, and physicians.

These astronauts have made history-making contributions participating in space shuttle missions to perform critical tasks such as deploying and retrieving satellites, performing spacewalks, conducting science and technology research, and commanding space shuttle missions. In 1987, engineer and physician, Mae C. Jemison became the first African-American woman accepted into NASA's astronaut training program, she was chosen out of a total of 2,000 applicants.

After a year of training, she became the first African-American woman astronaut to travel into space. She was selected to be a Science Mission Specialist aboard STS47 on the Space Shuttle Endeavor. The Science Mission Specialist was a new astronaut role being tested by NASA to focus on scientific experiments.

Jemison and six other crew members lifted off on their voyage into space on September 12, 1992. During her eight days in space, she conducted experiments on weightlessness and motion sickness on the crew as well as herself.

She spent more than 190 hours in space, while orbiting the earth a total of 127 times before returning from the mission. As a pioneer in space travel, Jemison went on to become an outspoken supporter of gender equality.

Following her historic flight, she noted that society should recognize how much both women and members of other minority groups can contribute if given the opportunity. After serving as an astronaut for six years, she retired from NASA in 1993. She then started "The Jemison Group," a consulting company that encourages students throughout the country to explore science, technology, and social change.

Known affectionately by her fans as "Flo-Jo," Florence Griffith-Joyner became the first woman to win four medals in Track and Field at a single Olympics, in the 1988 Seoul, Korea Games. Flo-Jo revolutionized women's sprinting with her searing speed and flamboyant fashion sense.

"Nothing is going to be handed to you. You have to make things happen."

-- *Florence Griffith-Joyner*

A decade after Black History Month had expanded as a month long celebration of African-American history in February, there were countless African-American athletes who emerged as record breakers and trendsetters. During the 1980's, track and field star, Florence Griffith Joyner captivated the world as she revolutionized women's sprinting with her lightning speed and flamboyant fashion sense.

Known affectionately by her fans as "Flo-Jo," she made speed fashionable, her racing attire consisted of a variety of fluorescent outfits bearing one leg and trademark four inch nails. In 1988, Flo-Jo arrived at the Olympic Games in Seoul, Korea as the favorite to win the 100 and 200 meter races. Just two months earlier, she obliterated the world record when she sprinted 100 meters in 10.49 seconds during the U.S. Olympic Trials, which is a record that still remains today.

As she competed in Seoul, Flo-Jo astounded the track and field world with another world-record performance that still remains today, as she sprinted 200 meters in 21.34 seconds. She won three gold medals in the 100 and 200 meter dashes, the 400-meter relay, and a silver in the 1600 meter relay. She became the first woman ever to win four medals in track and field at a single Olympics.

Her bold use of glamour in track and field changed the perception of beauty amongst all female athletes, she designed many of her outfits herself and preferred looks that were not conventional. Whether she was warming up, coming out of the block, running on the track or winning at the finish line, her glamorous appearance was always adored by fans.

Known as the "fastest woman in history," she became an important symbol of grace and beauty, she inspired all women across the globe to be the best at what they do. Flo-Jo remained a pop culture figure after her record-shattering performances and retirement from track and field, she signed a deal with toy maker LJN Toys for a Barbie-like doll in her likeness. Throughout her career she emerged as a cultural icon in track and field and changed the sport forever.

Known worldwide as a glamorous media mega-mogul, Oprah Winfrey has grown from a talk-show queen to the pinnacle of the entertainment universe. As a successful business owner, television and movie star, she is one of the greatest philanthropist in U.S. history. As her first name is one of the most recognizable brands in the world, she is the first African-American self-made billionaire.

"Think like a queen. A queen is not afraid to fail. Failure is another steppingstone to greatness."

-- *Oprah Winfrey*

During the mid-1980's, there were few African-American women on television with a national platform to discuss issues and events shaping the times. Shortly after winning a Miss Black Tennessee beauty pageant at the age of seventeen, Oprah Winfrey became the youngest and first African-American news anchor in Nashville at the age of nineteen. Soon after, she was recruited to co-anchor the six o'clock news at WJZ-TV in Baltimore, MD.

In 1986, Winfrey relocated to Chicago to host a low-rated half-hour morning talk show, AM Chicago. Within months, the show went from last place in the ratings, to the highest-rated talk show in Chicago. She expanded the program to an hour and named it the "Oprah Winfrey Show," which became the highest-rated television program in history, it ran in national syndication for 25 years, from 1986 to 2011. She then launched a cable channel, Oprah Winfrey Network (OWN).

Known as one of the greatest talk-show host ever, Winfrey also had a successful acting career, she has appeared in more than 30 motion picture and television roles. After launching a popular publication "O Magazine" and a production company, "Harpo," she developed documentaries, films, and broadway musicals. As a global media icon, her first name is one of the most recognizable brands in the world, she is also the first African-American self-made billionaire.

Winfrey has often used her platform, voice, and wealth to support social justice, she is also one of the greatest philanthropist in U.S. history. After establishing "The Oprah Winfrey Foundation," she has awarded hundreds of grants to organizations that support the education and empowerment of women, children and families around the world, she has also donated millions of dollars toward providing a better education for students who have merit but no means.

In 2007, she opened "The Oprah Winfrey Leadership Academy for Girls" (OWLAG) boarding school in South Africa. The school has transformed the lives of thousands of students, providing them with educational tools needed to realize their dreams of pursuing careers in fields such as medicine, architecture, and public service.

Computer Scientist and Engineer, Mark Dean was instrumental in the invention of the Personal Computer (PC). He is also responsible for the inception of the worlds first Gigahertz Chip. Dean holds three of IBM's original nine Personal Computer patents. His innovation allowed peripheral devices such as disk drives, monitors, printers, modems, and more to be plugged directly into computers, for better integrated and easier to use computing.

"A lot of kids growing up today aren't told that you can be whatever you want to be. There may be obstacles, but there are no limits."

-- *Mark Dean*

As more African-American innovators were being recognized for making technological advances during the 1970's and 1980's, computer scientist and engineer, Mark Dean developed a number of landmark technologies for IBM. Throughout his career, he pushed computer science and technology into a new era. In 1981, Dean was instrumental in the invention of the Personal Computer (PC), he also developed the color monitor for PC's.

During the time, the market for computers were meant for corporate, business, and governmental sectors. As a trailblazer, Dean made the personal computer more practical for everyday people.

The IBM personal computer, released in 1981, began with nine patents for its technology, three of which belonged specifically to Dean. He also invented the industry standard architecture system bus, which allows peripherals to plug-in to computers such as a mouse, printer, keyboard, or monitor.

Dean is one of the most prominent African-American inventors in the field of computers. His invention of the personal computer along with his improving the bus that made it possible for users to connect computers to peripherals by simply plugging them in, laid the foundation for the explosive growth in the computing industry worldwide.

Dean also developed a huge breakthrough at IBM and for the computer world as a whole, as he created the first one gigahertz computer processor chip in 1999. The revolutionary chip, tasked with carrying out the calculations and basic processes of a computer, was capable of doing one billion calculations per second, with this new technology, the computer world took a giant leap forward.

Dean's revolutionary work was rewarded at IBM as he became the first African-American to be awarded as an "IBM Fellow" (the highest honor for excellence at the company). Over the course of his career, he had more than 20 patents registered for his innovative computer engineering work, he later became Vice President at IBM and a member of the National Academy of Engineers.

Michelle Obama became the first African-American First Lady of the United States from 2009 to 2017, she is married to the 44th President of the United States, Barack Obama. She is also the most educated First Lady in American history, she skipped second grade, graduated Salutatorian at her magnet High School and has two Ivy League Degrees from Princeton and Harvard Law School.

"You cannot take your freedoms for granted. Just like generations who have come before you, you have to do your part to preserve and protect those freedoms, you need to be preparing yourself to add your voice to our national conversation."

-- *Michelle Obama*

Chapter 12 - Change Has Come

Three decades after Black History Month was established as an annual observance in the United States and three other countries, the first African-American President of the United States was elected into office. Michelle Obama officially became the first African-American "First Lady" when her husband Barack Obama was sworn in as the 44th President of the United States.

As the most educated First Lady in American history, Michelle was raised with an emphasis on education. After graduating from Princeton University in 1985, she went on to study law at Harvard Law School. After graduating law school in 1988, she relocated to her hometown of Chicago to work as a lawyer, joining the firm of Sidley Austin. She was then introduced to a young intern named Barack Obama, she was assigned to be his mentor and advisor. After years of dating, Barack and Michelle were married in 1992.

She helped her husband get elected to the U.S. Senate in 2004, she campaigned with him while trying to maintain a normal home life raising their two daughters Sasha and Malia. When Barack Obama ran for president in 2008, Michelle took a leave of absence from her job to help with the campaign, she played an integral role in the success of his political career as a Senator and President.

As the 44th First Lady of the United States from 2009 to 2017, Michelle was extremely effective in a number of her initiatives, which included her "Let's Move" program, which was a nationwide initiative to eliminate childhood obesity within a generation. Throughout her time in the White House she has also worked to support veterans and military families. Worldwide she has encouraged young people to continue with a higher education past high school, and attend a college or university. She has been voted as the most admired, as well as the most influential woman in the world for close to a decade after leaving the White House in 2017.

In 2009, President Barack Obama became the first African-American President of the United States of America. He was sworn in as the 44th President and took the oath of office using the same bible President Abraham Lincoln used when he was sworn in as President during his 1861 inauguration. Obama also became the first African-American to secure the nomination of any major national political party. He was also re-elected as President in 2012.

"Change will not come if we wait for some other person or some other time. We are the ones we've been waiting for. We are the change we seek."

-- *President Barack Obama*

In 1996, Barack Obama officially launched his political career, as he was elected to the Illinois State Senate, representing the South Side of Chicago Hyde Park neighborhood. He was then elected to the U.S. Senate in 2004. Prior to a career in public service, he was the first African-American president of the Harvard Law Review, he also taught constitutional law at the University of Chicago. As a community organizer, he worked as an attorney on civil rights issues.

Obama was a rising star within the National Democratic Party, speculation began about a Presidential future. He gained national recognition by delivering one of the greatest Keynote Addresses at the Democratic National Convention in July, 2004. The speech gave a personal narrative of Obama's biography with the theme that all Americans are connected in ways that transcend political, cultural, and geographical differences.

In 2008, he was elected as the first African-American President of the United States of America. His persona and charisma, along with his campaign promise to bring change to the established political system resonated with many Americans, especially young and minority voters. Obama was sworn in as president on January 20, 2009. His inauguration set an attendance record with two million people gathering at the U.S. Capital to bear witness to the historic event.

During his first term in office he signed some of his signature pieces of legislations, including "The Affordable Care Act," popularly known as "Obamacare," a new law giving every American citizen access to affordable healthcare. He also signed the American Recovery Act, which aimed to help the U.S. economy recover from a deepening worldwide recession. Obama was the first president to nominate and appoint two women to serve on the Supreme Court.

During his presidency, he was awarded the Nobel Peace Prize, for his extraordinary efforts to strengthen international diplomacy. In 2012, Obama was re-elected for a second term as President, his leadership continued as he ushered in a stronger U.S. economy, a more equal society, and a revitalized U.S. auto industry.

The National Museum of African-American History and Culture (NMAAHC) is the nation's largest and most comprehensive cultural destination devoted exclusively to exploring, documenting and showcasing the African-American story and its impact on American and world history. Established by an Act of Congress in 2003, the 400,000 square-foot museum is prominently located next to the Washington Monument and is the culmination of decades of efforts to establish a national museum that promotes and highlights the contributions of African-Americans.

Ninety years after Carter G. Woodson established an annual celebration known as Negro History Week, which later evolved into a monthly celebration in February known as Black History Month, the National Museum of African-American History and Culture (NMAAHC) located in Washington D.C. opened its doors to the public, making it the world's largest museum dedicated to African-American history and culture.

The NMAAHC was established by an Act of Congress in 2003, and opened its doors to the public on September 24, 2016, as the 19th museum of the Smithsonian Institution. The museum serves as a place where all Americans can learn about the richness and diversity of the African-American experience, and how it helped shape the nation.

The 10 story building (which 5 stories are below ground) houses more than 40,000 objects in its collection, visitors are able to explore more than four hundred years of artifacts and historical information.

For more than one hundred years, many advocates have pushed for a national museum to honor and explore the contributions of African-Americans. They had to overcome geographic and economic hurdles, fierce battles with Congress and multiple design challenges to make the dream possible.

The idea for the museum was first proposed by African-American veterans of the civil war one hundred years earlier. Following decades of lobbying, the highly anticipated museum finally came to fruition just in time as the nations first African-American President, Barack Obama presided over the grand opening before leaving office.

Since its opening, the NMAAHC has set new records as patrons spent an average of six hours viewing their many exhibits. The museum attracts over 3 million visitors every year, with an average of 8,000 people each day. The NMAAHC has become an essential stop for tourists visiting the nations capital, making it one of the most visited Smithsonian museums in the country.

In 2021, Vice President Kamala Harris became the first African-American Vice President of the United States of America. She served a lifetime of public service, having been elected as District Attorney of San Francisco, Attorney General of California, and a United States Senator. Serving as the 49th Vice President, she is the highest-ranking female official in U.S. history.

"I may be the first woman to hold this office. But I won't be the last."

-- *Vice President Kamala Harris*

As one of the most influential women in U.S. history, Kamala Harris has had many "firsts" in her life in public service. As a trailblazer, she was elected as the first African-American woman to serve in the United States Senate, representing the State of California. Harris was also the first African-American, and the first woman elected as District Attorney for the city of San Francisco, as well as the first African-American Attorney General for the State of California.

In 2020, she made history once again, as she was elected as the first African-American Vice President of the United States of America. After attending Howard University, then earning her law degree from Hastings College, Harris began her career in public service, as she was on a mission to changed the judicial system.

She began her career as a deputy district attorney in Oakland, California, she soon earned a reputation for her toughness as a prosecutor, and rose through the ranks to become district attorney in the city of San Francisco. She later broke through barriers as she became the first woman, and the first African-American elected as Attorney General of California.

In 2012, Harris delivered one of the most memorable speeches as she addressed the Democratic National Convention, raising her national profile. Widely considered a rising star within the party, she was encouraged to run for the U.S. Senate. In 2016, she became the first woman to win a Senate seat for California, becoming only the second African-American woman ever elected to the U.S. Senate.

When she took office in January 2017, she began serving on both the Select Committee on Intelligence and the Judiciary Committee, among other assignments, she was also a leading advocate for social-justice reform. As Harris achieved a number of historic milestones during her career, she shattered another glass ceiling as she was sworn in as Vice President on January 20, 2021. Serving as the 49th Vice President, she is the highest-ranking female official in U.S. history. Through her leadership, she continues to champion for millions of under-represented people all across the United States and the world.

As the month of February has marked the celebration of Negro History Week (1926) and Black History Month (1976) for close to a century, it has provided an amazing opportunity to celebrate and acknowledge the achievements of African-Americans throughout history. As a Harvard-trained historian, Dr. Carter G. Woodson believed that truth could not be denied, and reason would prevail over prejudice.

His hopes to raise awareness on African-American contributions was realized when he and the organization he founded in 1915, the Association for the Study of Negro Life and History, now called the Association for the Study of African-American Life and History (ASALH) conceived and announced Negro History Week.

The response since then has been overwhelming, by the time of Woodson's death in 1950, Black History Month has evolved into a cultural phenomenon that allows people from all cultures to learn more and understand the true history of the African Diaspora experience in America and across the world. The month of February has also allowed institutions to expand their curriculum and focus more on accurate and proper telling of African-American history.

Woodson believed that commemorations provide a kind of "real education," and inspires people to live more abundantly. As Black History Month was created to focus attention on the contributions of African-Americans, it also honors many unsung hero's for a period of over four hundred years.

While other countries such as Canada, the United Kingdom, Germany, and the Netherlands have joined the United States in bringing awareness to the many contributions that people of African descent made on the continent of Africa, The United States and the rest of the world, they have also created monthly celebrations similar to Black History Month.

As Woodson dedicated his life to telling the stories of African-Americans, he became known as the "Father of Black History." He is honored and remembered with numerous schools, parks, and buildings across the country bearing his name. His vision and legacy will last forever.

Sources

African-American Inventions That Changed The World: Today in African-American History: African-American Musicians That Changed Music Forever: Michael A. Carson. African-American Museum of History and Culture, Washington, D.C. National Association for the Advancement of Colored People (NAACP), The Association for the Study of African-American Life and History (ASALH) The Carter G. Woodson Collection: Negro History Week, The Education of The Negro Prior to 1861, The Mis-Education of the Negro, The correspondence of W. E. B. Du Bois, Volume 3. Carter G. Woodson, Father of Black History, United States Department of State, The History of Black History Month, National Inventors Hall of Fame, African-American Athletes, Chronology of African-American History, Professional Baseball Hall of Fame, Nobel Peace Price Archives, Boxing Hall of Fame, Screen Actors Guild, Phillis Wheatley: Poems on Various Subjects, Religious and Moral The Caudron Brother's School of Aviation, Academy Award Archives, Major League Baseball Hall of Fame, The United States Armed Forces, The United States Supreme Court, Tennis Hall of Fame, International Women's Sports Hall of Fame, Rock & Roll Hall of Fame, Black Wall Street Archives, Madame C.J. Walker's Wonderful Hair Grower Bethune-Cookman University Archives, Tuskegee Airmen, the 332nd Fighter Group and the Red Tails, National Aeronautics and Space Administration (NASA).

How Did Black History Month Begin?

ACKNOWLEDGMENTS

As always, I have to begin by giving thanks to God, for guiding my life and giving my family and I his infinite blessings.

To my lovely wife Shenika and our son Matthew.

To my parents, Mary and Sam, who gave me life and taught me how to love God and Family.

To my sister and brother-in-law, Sandra and Arthur. To my brother and sister-in-law, Sanford and Brigette. Thank you for your love and support.

To my nieces and nephews, Serena, Stephanie, Shayla, Jayda, Keiana, Darin, Darius and Austin.

To the entire Carson, Street, Hall and Bolden families. Much love to all of you.

ABOUT THE AUTHORS

Michael and Matthew Carson are a Best-Selling, Award-Winning Father and Son writing team. They are most well known for their publications: "African-American Inventions That Changed The World," "Today In African-American History," "African-American Musicians That Changed Music Forever," and "Unknown African-American History Makers."

Growing up in Queens, New York, Michael has a Bachelor's Degree in Psychology from Virginia State University and works as a Government Analyst. Matthew is a student who enjoys researching and writing about history. Their family currently resides in Atlanta, Georgia.

What began as a conversation with Michael teaching his son Matthew about African-American history, continued into a five book non-fiction series. Together their passion for learning about historical figures grew into a collaboration, and they wanted to educate future generations about the many significant contributions African-Americans have made in our society and the world.

Michael and his wife Shenika co-founded Double Infinity Publishing. Their goal is to publish high quality literature that represents historical facts as well as provide a voice and platform for educating readers.

www.ingramcontent.com/pod-product-compliance
Lightning Source LLC
Chambersburg PA
CBHW081233090426
42738CB00016B/3286